The Organized Life

SECRETS OF AN EXPERT ORGANIZER

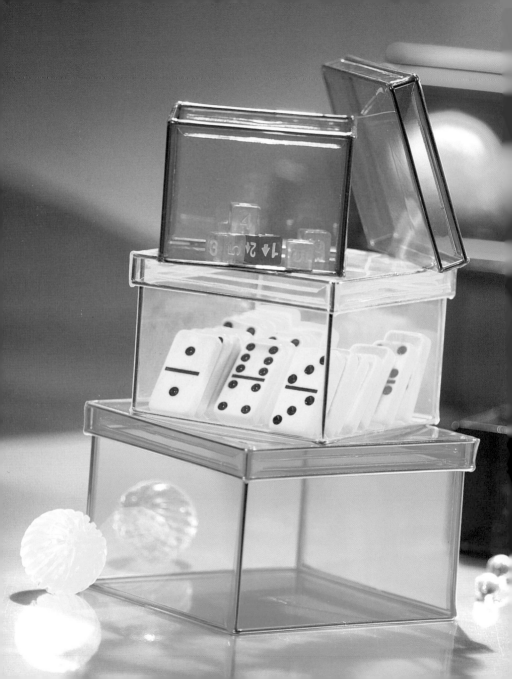

The Organized Life

SECRETS OF AN EXPERT ORGANIZER

STEPHANIE DENTON

NORTH LIGHT BOOKS
Cincinnati, Ohio

Published by North Light Books, an imprint of F+W Publications, Inc., 4700 E. Galbraith Rd., Cincinnati, Ohio, 45236. Tel: (800) 289-0963. First edition.

Other fine North Light Books are available from your local bookstore or direct from the publisher.

10 09 08 07 06   5 4 3 2

Distributed in Canada by Fraser Direct, 100 Armstrong Avenue, Georgetown, ON, Canada, L7G 5S4. Tel: (905) 877-4411

Distributed in the U.K. and Europe by David & Charles, Brunel House, Newton Abbot, Devon, TQ12 4PU, England. Tel: (+44) 1626 323200, Fax: (+44) 1626 323319, E-mail: postmaster@davidandcharles.co.uk

Distributed in Australia by Capricorn Link, P.O. Box 704, S. Windsor NSW, 2756 Australia. Tel: (02) 4577-3555

Library of Congress Cataloging-in-Publication Data
Denton, Stephanie
  The organized life: Secrets of an expert organizer / by Stephanie Denton.– 1st ed.
    p. cm.
  Includes index.
  ISBN-13: 978-1-58180-863-6 (alk. paper)
  ISBN-10: 1-58180-863-1 (alk. paper)
  1. Storage in the home. 2. House cleaning. I. Title.
  TX309.D42 2006
  648'.8–dc22   2006006736

Editor: Kathy Kipp
Production Editor: Vanessa Lyman
Designer: Clare Finney
Production Coordinator: Greg Nock
Photographer: Tim Grondin

ABOUT THE AUTHOR

Stephanie Denton is an organizing and productivity expert who has been featured on the front pages of both *The Wall Street Journal* and *USA Today*. Her clients include individuals, small businesses and corporations such as Johnson & Johnson and Procter & Gamble. She is also an advisor to major organizing product manufacturers and retailers.

Stephanie is a syndicated newspaper columnist and a frequent contributor to national magazines. She has been interviewed hundreds of times on television and news programs around the country and by such publications as *The New York Times*, *Business Week*, *Inc.*, *Reader's Digest*, *Family Circle*, *Real Simple*, *Better Homes & Gardens* and *Entrepreneur*.

Stephanie is past president of the National Association of Professional Organizers and a recipient of its prestigious Founders Award, the industry's highest award for career achievements and industry contributions.

DEDICATION

To those who have given me opportunities, taught me excellence and believed in me: MDD, JKD, ADC, ECB, SLS and P.

ACKNOWLEDGMENTS

With thanks to those who worked in the past and the present to make this book possible: Kathy Kipp, Clare Finney, Ivan Hoffman and Paulette Ensign.

contents

The Organized Life

Being organized is about living the life you want to live. It's more than creating a beautiful space or getting things done fast, although both are extremely valuable results of getting organized. Being organized is about reaching for your dreams and having an environment that supports your doing so.

This book is a compilation of real life solutions that have worked best for my clients over the years. It includes both big picture concepts and detailed explanations: new ways of thinking that apply in many situations and specific suggestions for common hot spots.

If you feel overwhelmed by all of the information and opportunities you're faced with each day, this book is for you. Choose just one of the solutions to implement and you'll find it can make a difference. Let this book inform and inspire you to create your organized life.

1 Clutter

Clutter can be defined as whatever gets in your way. Sometimes it's stuff that needs to be put away, other times it's stuff that needs to be thrown away, and it can even take the form of commitments and responsibilities that you should let go.

When you get rid of the clutter, you have space for your dreams to come true. What do you want to make room for in your life? Stay focused on the reward and you'll stay motivated throughout the process.

"Keep only what is beautiful, useful or loved."

When you are sorting through your stuff, sometimes it's hard to decide if an item should stay or go. Ask yourself these questions:

1. Is it beautiful?

2. Is it useful?

3. Is it loved?

If you answered "yes" to any of these questions, it should stay. If the answer is "no" to all three, it can probably go.

The cost of clutter

How much has clutter cost you?

* Have you ever incurred late fees and interest charges because you paid a bill after the due date?

* Have you ever bought a duplicate tool because you couldn't find the one you had or forgot you even owned it?

* Have you paid a premium to mail a package at the last minute?

* Did you have to keep a purchase you decided you didn't want, just because the store's return cutoff date had already passed?

* Have your good clothes ever been ruined by moth holes because they weren't stored appropriately?

* Have you ever missed a tax deduction because you misplaced a charitable donation record?

* Has food that's been pushed to the back of your refrigerator spoiled before you could eat it?

* Have you ever been unable to get a product repaired at no charge, despite warranty, because you couldn't find the receipt?

* Do you have a rented storage unit holding your extra furniture?

When you add up the dollar amounts, you can see that clutter hits you hard in the pocketbook. Isn't it worth spending time getting organized?

✳ **Target** the room that would be most valuable to you if it was organized. Frequently, this is where you spend the most time.

✳ **Start** with what's most current. In the kitchen, for example, the papers on top of the island are probably both recent and important to you. Get those in order first. As additional mail or kids' papers arrive each day, incorporate them into your new system. Once your new process is working smoothly, you can tackle the backlog of older paper.

✳ **Consider** your garbage can, recycling bin and donation box your top organizing tools. The larger they are, the more likely you are to use them.

✳ **Create** a donation directory to encourage quick disposal of excess items. List your favorite local charities and include phone number, hours of operation, articles accepted and the drop off/pickup policy.

✳ **Purge** once a year. What was useful at one time in your life, might not be anymore.

Three-box strategy

Familiar with the 80/20 rule? It applies to clutter, too. You use twenty percent of your stuff eighty percent of the time. However, it's mentally and physically difficult to get rid of the unused portion in one swoop. Instead, use the "three-box strategy" to whittle clutter away.

1. Label three cardboard boxes: "Keep," "Not Sure" and "Toss."

2. Quickly sort items into the appropriate boxes. It will be easy to decide what belongs in the "Keep" and "Toss" boxes.

3. Whenever an item slows you down, that's your cue it belongs in the "Not Sure" box.

4. When you finish this rapid sort, put the "Keep" items back where they belong.

5. Get rid of whatever landed in "Toss"—donate, sell or give it away.

6. Steer clear of this area for a week.

7. Return and repeat the process with the "Not Sure" items. You'll find you're mentally ready to put some of last week's "Not Sure" into the "Toss" box.

8. Use the process as many times as necessary until you're satisfied with the amount you've discarded.

Bit by bit

When organizing, commit to a single area or pile that you can complete within the time available. When you finish that assignment, you can stop for the day. Of course, if you are motivated to continue, fine. But don't feel guilty if you wrap up—you only committed yourself to that one job. When you're ready, select another area and tackle it. Gradually you'll work your way through the entire house. Remember, any big project is only the sum of several small projects.

After you've been working for a while, your space may look like a train wreck. Don't worry—you haven't derailed. When you're organizing a cluttered space, it always looks worse before it gets better.

4 ways to condense a collection

How can you preserve the memory without the possession? Shrink the collection, keeping just enough for reminiscence.

✳ **TAKE PHOTOS.** Pictures of your child grinning by his oversized art projects look great in an album of his school years. The actual projects can be discarded.

✳ **SAVE ONLY A REPRESENTATIVE SAMPLE.** Are you storing your first set of dishes in the attic even though you'll never use them again? Hang one plate decoratively on the kitchen wall.

✳ **CREATE A NEW OBJECT.** Cut swatches from favorite clothes—anything from a beloved T-shirt to your children's baby clothes—and work them into a quilt.

✳ **INDEX IT.** If you no longer want a library of books in your home, but want to remember what you had, create an index of your collection. Donate the books and refer to the index if you want to recall a book you had. Then order it from the public library.

Duplicates that make sense

As a general rule, getting organized involves getting rid of things. But sometimes it's actually more efficient to have more than one of an item, each stored at the point of use.

VACUUM CLEANER	Store the big vacuum cleaner where you use it most often. Place a handheld vacuum in places that frequently call for quick pickups.
OFFICE SUPPLIES	Keep extra office supplies (tape, scissors) in each room of the house in which you use them. Label by room so they don't end up in other places.
LAUNDRY BASKETS	Have two laundry baskets so you—or your kids—can sort between whites and colors as you go and avoid that process later.
SUN GLASSES	Buy a second pair of sunglasses to keep exclusively in your car. An extra compact umbrella is handy to have in the glove compartment.

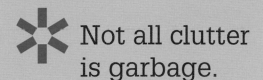

Not all clutter is garbage.

Sometimes the chaos is simply a matter of prized possessions being out of place.

START A NEW HABIT. Whenever you're holding an item, don't put it down unless you're returning it to its home. This doesn't mean you have to pick up everything strewn around your house right now. But the next time you have something in your hand, don't set it back down "just anywhere."

When you're decluttering, be sure there's enough light.

You'll sort faster and be more motivated in a bright area. If you have to strain to see, the process can quickly become frustrating. It's okay to turn on your favorite music; however, stay away from separating clutter while watching TV because it's too easy to get distracted.

Get yourself a clutter buddy

For extra encouragement on a big job, ask a friend to be your clutter buddy. Offer to spend time organizing at her house if she'll devote an afternoon to helping you sort through your stuff. When a partner is helping, you can focus your energy on deciding what to keep and what to toss.

1. Select the area in which you will work. You'll need a work surface and a chair. Bring them in from another room if necessary.

2. Stay seated while your clutter buddy brings you items to evaluate. The goal is for you to have a constant, steady stream of objects to review.

3. She should pre-sort for you, gathering like objects from around the room and showing you all of them at once.

4. Pay attention to your energy levels. As necessary, have your buddy alternate between bringing you no-brainers or bulky items that can be decided on quickly and will make a big physical impact (such as a broken popcorn popper), and those that may require more individual, thoughtful attention (such as a pile of Christmas cards received over the years).

5. Once you make a decision, it's your buddy's job to physically deal with the item—for example, to place kitchen gadgets in a donation box, shred discarded papers or hang a garment back in your closet.

BOTTOM LINE. You make all the decisions and aren't slowed down by the physical work. Your partner makes no decisions but does the physical work.

Worried that...

you "might need it someday"?

If you keep everything you *might* need someday, you're going to need a warehouse. If everything seems potentially useful, maybe you're not sure what's truly important to you. Think about your hopes and dreams. Then identify what items or information will support you in achieving them. Without knowing this, *all* of your stuff can seem worthwhile.

 Avoid creating a new goal to justify each piece of clutter.

Worried that...

you "paid good money for it"?

Just because you bought something doesn't mean you have to keep it forever. If you used it, you already received some return on your investment. If you didn't, it's okay to admit it was a mistake and move on. In reality, getting rid of the item (by donating it and taking a tax deduction or by selling or consigning it) is the only way to recoup some of the money you've already spent and are continuing to spend in order to house it.

 If you're not using an item, it's not paying you back.

Worried that...

they "don't make them like this anymore"?

There may be a reason for that. Product improvements often render earlier generations obsolete. Have you used it in the past two years? If so, fine. But if you're holding on just because you can't replace it with a comparable item, it's only wasting space. You can acknowledge the workmanship while also admitting it doesn't have a place in your life anymore. Someone else may appreciate it and put it to use.

> Discarding an item does not mean you are overlooking or disrespecting its quality.

Worried that…

you'll have to "get rid of all your memories"?

Getting organized is not about throwing away your memories. But it's hard to relax when keepsakes compete for your attention from every direction. If you're saving something because it holds a special memory for you, double check whether there's another way to reminisce. Does some other object prompt similar emotions? Consider this: what if giving away an item would *enhance* its significance? Share your cherished possessions now with younger generations and see them come alive again.

 Too many "memory joggers" create mental clutter.

"Never buy something just because it's on sale;

never accept something just because it's free."

You will pay a price later in terms of storage space, frustration from clutter and difficulty in parting with it. Considering these financial and emotional costs, it may be more expensive than you first thought.

Who says it's clutter?

Years ago I worked with a client who had four complete sets of picnic furniture in her garage— tables, chairs, the works. If you didn't know any better, you'd think this was clutter. But if you spent time talking with her, you learned that she was a single mother with a teenage daughter. She wanted her daughter to feel comfortable being in their home and having her friends over. So everything from the end-of-the-school-year party to the soccer team picnic was held at her house. With each event, all of that furniture was brought out of the garage and set up on the lawn. It wasn't a case of "I might need it someday." She used it on a routine basis and doing so was directly related to accomplishing one of her most important goals: being involved in her daughter's life. Even though there was a lot of picnic furniture, it certainly wasn't clutter.

2 Paper

If you're like many people, you find paper to be over-whelming. It piles into your life each day, seemingly from every direction. The mailman brings it, kids carry it home from school, you get handouts at meetings and appointments, and you print information from the internet.

While there is more information both available to you and sent to you than ever before, it is possible to get it all under control. Once you put simple processes in place, making decisions about what to do with paper and acting on them will be a snap. In no time at all, you'll have clear surfaces. You'll be able to find information quickly. Best of all, you'll have time to take advantage of all the opportunities these papers represent.

A BONUS: The same organizing principles that work for paper will also help you manage electronic information.

Here, there and everywhere

Does this describe your paper clutter? Defeat the disorder by establishing an official paper management center in your home. This can be a home office or a work surface in another room. After all, you have a specific place for activities such as cooking and sleeping. Why not one for processing and storing paper?

"Use your inbox to hold only things you haven't looked at yet."

Use an inbox or basket to hold new mail until you have time to open it. You'll prevent piles from forming on the kitchen counter, coffee table and bedroom chair.

Choose a convenient location for your inbox. If you collect mail at the front door, place a basket on a table in the entry hall. If you bring mail in through the garage, corral incoming information near this entrance.

Put all unopened mail in your inbox so you'll know where it is when you're ready to read it.

Avoid reviewing the papers in the inbox, saying to yourself, "I know what I need to do with these," but then leaving them there. You'll just have to spend time sorting again later. Once you take a paper out of the inbox, move it forward in some way: pitch it, give it to someone else, file it or act on it.

Sorting through a big stack

Just the sight of their desk littered with paper is enough to send some people in the other direction. Instead of avoiding the situation, use this simple process to whittle down a large pile.

1. Gather the papers that are strewn about. Square them into a neat stack. If there's a lot, you may need to create two or three stacks.

2. Pull out thick documents. Examples include catalogs, magazines and phone directories. Put these large items away or discard them. This will shorten the stack significantly and produce immediate visual results.

3. Sort the papers remaining in the stack, dividing them into two piles: "Keep" and "Pitch."

4. Focus your attention on how much can go into the "Pitch" pile. For now, don't worry about the "Keep" papers, and refrain from sorting them into additional piles; organizing them is a separate process.

5. Once you've gone through everything, put the "Pitch" pile in the garbage can or recycling bin.

6. Go back through the "Keep" pile. Are you willing to part with more? A second pass is usually worth it; once you've looked at all the papers and pitched some, you begin to realize how little you really need.

"The larger your garbage can, the more likely you are to use it."

FLIP IT. The oldest papers are usually easiest to get rid of and are frequently at the bottom of any pile. If your accumulation has been building for a while, turn it over and deal with the bottom papers first. You'll gain momentum for tackling the rest.

How to get rid of more paper

Most filed paper is never looked at again. Think about your own files. What percent would you say you've referred to in the past two years? If you're having trouble paring down, asking yourself these questions can prompt you to pitch more than you might otherwise. They're helpful both when clearing out old files and evaluating new mail.

QUESTION	KEEP IN MIND
Can I state the specific circumstance in which this information would be useful?	Thinking you might need a paper someday isn't a reason to keep it. Do so only if you know exactly when you'd need it—such as a financial record that would be needed during a tax audit.
How hard would it be for me to get this information again later, when and if I actually need it?	If you'd be able to retrieve the information easily, chances are less likely that you need to keep a hard copy now.
Is the information recent enough to be useful?	What was once good information may now be outdated.
Is holding on to this piece of paper getting me any closer to realizing one of my dreams?	If it's not in line with your priorities, then it's not only cluttering your desk, it's cluttering your mind.

ALL PAPERS FALL INTO ONE OF THESE TWO HEADINGS:

Active papers. These are ones you need to act on

or access frequently. Examples include current projects, bills
to pay, school phone lists.

Reference papers. These require no action,

except retaining them for future reference. Examples include
completed projects, medical records and tax files.

Most people physically group files into categories
(such as insurance, school, children). But a more effective strategy is to first divide them between active
and reference. This way, all of the active files—the
ones needing your attention—will be together. Within
the active and reference divisions, you can then subdivide by category.

Store your active files close at hand. Use the file
drawer in your desk or a desktop file rack. Reference
information can be kept in a cabinet elsewhere or even
in another room if you're short on space. (For space
planning purposes, note that it's not unusual to have
up to ten times more reference files than active files.)

When it's obvious to you where a piece of paper should be filed, it's quick to put it away. It's also fast to find it again later because there's no question about where you would have put it.

Other times, you may not be immediately sure where a paper belongs. In these instances, it's tempting to make a case for putting it "somewhere" just to get it off your desk. This is dangerous, however, because you're likely to forget the rationalization you used and thus forget where the paper is.

Instead, ask yourself this question: "If I were searching for this today in my file cabinet, what is the first folder in which I would look?" The answer to that question tells you where you should file the paper. Six months from now, when you are looking for that document, your brain will use the same thought process to locate it.

Options for Paper

Paper you haven't looked at belongs in your inbox. Once you take it out of the inbox and review it, you have only four options for what to do with it. The option you choose dictates where the paper belongs.

HOW YOU DESCRIBE THE PAPER	WHAT YOU SHOULD DO	WHERE IT BELONGS
I don't need this.	Toss it.	Garbage can or recycling bin.
Someone else is better qualified to handle this.	Give it to someone else.	Outbox.
I need to hold onto this for potential future reference.	File it.	Reference files.
I need to do something with this.	Add a reminder to your to-do list. Then file it.	Action files.

These four options work for e-mail as well. After all, in your electronic system you have an inbox, a recycle bin, an outbox and the ability to create folders and file messages accordingly.

Create a file index

This is a list of your files that serves as a "table of contents" for your filing cabinets. When you're looking for a particular file, scan the index to see where it is. You won't have to open every drawer to find what you want. Also review the index before creating a new file. This will prevent you from starting a new folder called "school" when you already have one labeled "education."

What to do with miscellaneous paper

When it's not clear where a paper should be filed, it's tempting to dump it into a "miscellaneous" file. But you may forget what's in there and miss important deadlines. A better solution is to set up a "tickler" file. This is an organized, temporary holding place for papers that don't fit into your current filing system and yet don't justify the creation of a new permanent file. Just like a calendar is where you would write future appointments, a "tickler" file is where you would store the seemingly miscellaneous paper you'll need in the future.

1. Fill a file drawer near your desk with 43 hanging file folders.

2. Label the first 31 folders with the numbers 1 through 31 and the remaining 12 folders with the months January through December.

3. When you receive a paper you don't need until later in the same month, put it in the appropriate 1 through 31 folder. For example, information for a field trip on the 17th goes into folder 17.

4. When you receive a paper you don't need until later in the year, put it in the folder for the month you'll need it. For example, plane tickets for July go into the July folder.

5. At the beginning of each month, sort the papers from that month's folder into the appropriate 1 through 31 folders.

6. Each morning (or the night before, if your mornings tend to be hectic), pull out the papers for that date. You will feel confident that nothing has been forgotten or misplaced.

Use yellow sticky notes to capture information you'll need only temporarily. Don't put information on them that you should be writing in a permanent record. After all, if you don't have time to write it in the right location in the first place, when are you going to find time to copy it over?

Quick file tips

Sometimes the simplest ideas make the biggest difference. Here are easy ways to make your files work better.

- Use clear tabs on hanging file folders, not colored ones. It's easier to read the label inside.

- The best way to create legible labels is to use a computer or hand-held label-making device. The second best option is to use a dark marker and write in large letters. Avoid writing lightly in pencil. It's just too hard to read from a distance.

- Put the tab on the front flap of the hanging folder, not the back one. No more push-pull motion; just grab the tab and pull the folder toward you to open. Plus, the file contents won't stick up and block the label.

- Use manila folders inside hanging file folders *only* when there's a clear need to subdivide the information. Otherwise, they create unnecessary bulk.

- If you must subdivide, use *interior* manila folders. They're cut slightly shorter than regular manila folders and don't block the tabs on hanging folders.

- Remove paperclips before filing papers. They can fall off or get stuck on other documents. Staple papers instead.

Color-code your files

There are many benefits to using the great-looking colored file folders and labels that are available, including the fact that:

* Colored folders are bright and attractive. If you are motivated by aesthetics, having visually appealing files is important.

* You can use color to differentiate between different categories or types of files.

* Folders are less likely to be misfiled because it's obvious if you mistakenly insert one color folder in the midst of several of another color.

Just be sure not to make your system too complicated. If you use a lot of different colors or your system is overly complex:

* It will be difficult to remember the code.

* You may spend inordinate amounts of time deciding what color a new file should be.

* You'll have to keep many boxes of different folder colors on hand. Otherwise, if you need to start a new file and you're out of the necessary color, you may end up piling the paper instead of filing it.

Three-ring binders are a good choice

for papers that must be kept in chronological order or ones you frequently carry with you to meetings and appointments. However, think carefully before using binders for any other paper storage. They occupy a fixed amount of room even if they contain only a single sheet. Their capacity is finite. Plus, you have to punch holes in all your paper. Folders offer more flexibility.

Cut down on catalog and magazine clutter

Prevent publications from overtaking your house with these strategies:

- **ARRANGE** catalogs in an upright rack or basket rather than piling them. It will be easier to riffle through, find the old version and replace it when the new one arrives.

- **WANT TO BE SURE** you don't discard catalogs from which you're considering placing an order? Use paper clips, not folded pages, to indicate potential purchases so these catalogs will be easier to spot. You could also rip out the page and staple it to the order form, then toss the catalog.

- **CUT DOWN** on catalog chaos by requesting that retailers not share your name and address with other companies. Look for a check box on the paper or online order form to indicate this preference.

- **EVALUATE** the value of the free magazines and newsletters you receive from clubs and organizations to which you belong. If you had to pay cash for these publications, would you? If they're not worth paying for, they're not worth your time to read. Recycle them as soon as they arrive or ask to be removed from the distribution list.

- **HESITANT** to part with glossy decorating magazines because you "paid good money for them"? Realize that once you've read them, you've received your money's worth of information and they can go. If there are a few pages you want to keep, tear them out and file them.

Can getting organized make you rich?

Working together with clients to get their paper and information in order, I've uncovered stock certificates in a closet, uncashed checks in a drawer and hundreds of dollars in cash in a file folder. Some clients knew they were missing this money and were looking for it. Others had forgotten it even existed. Either way, each time it happened it was a great testimonial to how it pays to get organized. (*Now* do you want to address that cardboard box of papers stashed in the corner?)

Even if you don't find cold, hard cash, organizing your information has many other financial benefits. You can avoid late fees and interest charges on bills. You can track your investment portfolio more closely. You can have appliances and products repaired while they're still under warranty. You can file insurance claims in a timely manner. You can get refunds and rebates you're entitled to. You can save money on office supplies because you have less paper to store. And so forth. You get the picture.

Most valuable, however, is the benefit that is hard to put a dollar figure on. When you're organized in a way that works for you, you can focus your energy on living the life you want to live. What is that worth to you?

3 Closets

A closet full of clothes and shoes represents a large financial investment. Maximize your return on this investment by organizing your garments so they are protected
from dirt and damage and you can get to them easily.
When you can see what you have, you are more likely to
mix and match, resulting in countless new outfits. Skip
the mall and go shopping in your newly organized closet
for free!

You'll get an emotional benefit too. Opening the door to
a well-ordered closet is a peaceful way to start the day.
Select an outfit that makes you look fabulous and you'll
not only feel good, you'll also make a great impression
on the people you meet throughout the day.

Compartmentalize your closet

Make your closet work for you by dividing it into "compartments," creating specific sections for different categories of clothing.

✳ Good. Do this at no cost by simply rearranging what's in your closet. It's faster to find your favorite pair of pants, for example, if all of your trousers are hanging together on the rod than if they're interspersed with other garments. Sort further within each category by hanging clothes of the same color together.

✳ Better. Use closet accessories to define your space. Hang a vertical sweater sorter from the rod. Place a shoe cubby between the bottom of your short garments (shirts, jackets) and the floor. Purchase a "double hang bar," (a wooden bar suspended from metal posts that hook over your existing closet rod) to create additional hanging space.

✳ Best. Install a custom closet that physically divides your space into distinct areas for different kinds of garments. Use an adjustable system so it can be reconfigured if your needs change. Have a professional closet company put it in for you or purchase components you can install yourself.

The fastest way to put your closet in order is to switch to one standard hanger style and turn all clothes facing the same direction.

PLASTIC, PADDED OR WOODEN HANGERS are much kinder to your clothes than wire ones. Plus, if you use thicker hangers, you won't be able to fit as much into your closet. This can be just the prompting you need to weed out what you don't wear!

USE HANGERS WITH TOPS THAT SWIVEL. No matter which way items are placed on the hanger, it will still be easy to hang clothes all facing one way.

CORRAL EMPTY HANGERS IN ONE PLACE. When you take an item off a hanger, put that hanger at the end of the rod. You'll always be able to find an available one when you need it.

Use shoulder covers to protect expensive clothes

❋ Available in fabric or vinyl, these low-cost items cover the top six to eight inches of a hanging garment and keep it free of dust.

❋ They also keep your clothes clean in the event you are flipping through your closet with dirt or makeup on your hands.

❋ Find them at storage and organization stores, mass merchants or online. If you prefer to sew your own, use unbleached, natural cotton fabric.

❋ They're a better option than a dry cleaner's bag, which tears easily, doesn't ventilate as well, and prevents getting items on and off the hanger with ease because of its length.

Access your accessories

You are more likely to wear belts and scarves if you can see them. Storage options include:

✳ Suspending them on individual hooks screwed into the back of the closet door.

✳ Rolling and placing them in a clear, multi-pocket footwear bag.

✳ Hanging them on a slide-out rack mounted to the closet wall.

✳ Using a hanger-style organizer stored alongside your clothes.

✳ If you have jewelry that goes with only one outfit, put it in a resealable bag and fasten the bag to the hanger holding that ensemble.

Double your hanging space

Most closets have just one rod, approximately 65 to 69 inches (165 to 175 cm) above the floor. If you want to raise it and add a second rod below, follow these steps:

1. Reposition the first rod at a height between 76 and 84 inches (193 to 213 cm) above the floor.

2. Add a lower rod between 36 and 42 inches (91 and 107 cm) from the floor.

The above measurements are guidelines. Let the height and shape of your closet, as well as your personal height, determine exactly where to place the rods. Just be sure your configuration allows enough space between the rods for these items

ITEM OF CLOTHING	SPACE BETWEEN RODS
Shirts and tops	28 inches (71 cm)
Women's suits	29 inches (74 cm)
Men's suits	38 inches (1 meter)
Pants folded over a hanger	20 inches (51 cm)

How far forward to install a closet rod

Position your rod far enough from the back of the closet that hangers don't bump into the wall. If you use standard-size hangers, the rod should be between 12 and 14 inches (31 cm and 36 cm) from the back wall. If you use oversized hangers, carefully measure where the rod should go. You need to be able to slide garments easily along the rod without scraping the back wall, but you also need to be able to close the door to the closet.

For coat closets, allow a little extra space for bulky winter coats and men's overcoats, which are wider at the shoulders to accommodate their suit jackets.

Reinvent the laundry bag

HANG A DRAWSTRING BAG on the back of the closet door. When a garment is ready for the dry cleaner's, place it in the bag. Once a week, drop it off when running errands, or call for pickup if your dry cleaner offers that service. You'll prevent the disappointment of planning to wear an outfit, only to realize it isn't presentable.

HOOK A MESH BAG to the edge of your laundry basket. Put stockings and lingerie in there to be washed. When it's full, you'll know it's time to launder the delicates. Separate lights from darks, place one load back in the mesh bag and drop into your washing machine's gentle cycle. Another option is to handwash them in the sink.

Old place, no space

Many old houses have tiny or awkwardly shaped closets. If you're dealing with these limitations, here are ideas and options to keep in mind:

- Instead of keeping everything in one closet, you may need to divide your clothes and store some in other clearly defined areas. You can organize by item (dresses here, shoes there) or by use (professional clothes in the closet, weekend wear in a dresser).

- Use freestanding storage pieces, such as armoires, as extensions of your closet. Some armoires can even be converted to have both hanging and shelf space.

- If you don't have too many long hanging clothes, you can move a small dresser into the closet underneath the high rod. This also opens up some space in the bedroom.

- Bedroom wall space is often overlooked. Install rows of hooks or Shaker-style pegs to provide an easy way to keep things off the floor. This works well for nightgowns and robes as well as casual T-shirts and pants.

- Be vigilant about rotating clothes seasonally so you're not cluttering the closet with anything that can't be worn at the moment. Or, make it a point to buy clothing that can be worn in any season.

- If you're lucky and have a small extra bedroom in the house, convert this entire room into a walk-in closet.

Shoe storage

Protect the investment you have in your shoes by storing them carefully instead of jumbling them on the floor. Here are some inexpensive options:

OPTION	WHEN TO USE
Wooden shoe cubby.	When you have empty floor space.
Hanging multi-pocket organizer.	When the back of the closet door is available.
Vertical sorter that hooks over closet rod.	When clothing doesn't take up all your hanging space.
Rolling under-the-bed organizer.	When the closet is full.
Stacking racks.	When you want flexibility in how many pairs you can store.

If you prefer to store your shoes in boxes, either the original ones or clear plastic replacements, take a photo of each pair of shoes and tape it to the end of its box. When they're stacked on shelves, you'll have a visual inventory of your collection.

❋ Most people wear twenty percent of their clothes eighty percent of the time.

It would be unrealistic to get rid of that unused majority all at once. Instead, clean out your closet progressively. Start at one end. Look at each garment and assign it to one of three categories:

1. **KEEP.** The "keep" items that should stay in your closet are those that you wear often. You may find special occasion and sentimentally significant items that you also want to hold onto. Identify a separate storage space for these so your closet isn't so full.

2. **NEEDS WORK.** Have two boxes on hand to collect items that need repair/alterations or cleaning. If this work must be done professionally, take the full boxes to your car and make trips to the tailor and dry cleaner. Otherwise, distribute the contents to the appropriate places in your house, such as your sewing room or laundry center.

3. **ELIMINATE.** Don't like it? Doesn't fit? Haven't worn it in the last two years? Donate articles in good condition to charity, consign them or put into a garage sale. Toss out the others. There's no sense in keeping something you're not drawn to.

Once you've made a first pass through the entire closet, repeat the process a week later. See if you can identify some additional discards. Most people find they are willing to pare down further.

Use it or lose it

Here's a way to track, on an ongoing basis, which clothes you wear and which you tend to ignore. Turn the hangers backward over the rod for items you suspect are worn infrequently. If you pull a garment off and wear it, turn the hanger around properly. Soon it will be easy to spot clothes that aren't getting much use because their hangers will still be backwards.

"The less you have, the less you have to organize."

IF YOU'RE LIKE MANY, you hesitate to get rid of clothing (even if you don't actually wear it) because of what you spent on it. You feel extra twinges of guilt about a garment that still has the original tags on it. What you may not realize is that it's still costing you now. It's costing you in closet space, in remorse and in the amount of frustration you feel when you can't find something you're looking for in your jam-packed closet.

So why not donate it so that someone who truly needs it can use it? In the future, consider the financial cost of storage space and emotional cost of disarray before buying an outfit—even if it seems like a great bargain at the time. Limit your purchases to those items that really make you feel good about yourself when you try them on.

4 steps to protecting out-of-season clothing

1. **CLEAN.** Every item should be washed or dry cleaned. Food, makeup and other stains (even invisible ones) can entice insects that may damage clothing. Also, this cleaning will remove any microscopic insect eggs that may already be in the fabric.

2. **STORE.** Cardboard boxes attract insects and can cause permanent color changes in certain fabrics. Instead, store clothing in garment bags, boxes or chests that allow the articles to "breathe" but keep out sunlight and dust.

3. **PROTECT.** Cedar's aroma helps prevent adult moths from coming in and laying eggs. Rejuvenate old cedar products by sanding the surface or freshening with a commercial cedar spray. Here's a rule of thumb: if you can smell the cedar fragrance in your storage container, it's probably strong enough to be effective. Some herbal sachets provide similar protection with a different scent.

4. **PLACE.** Avoid storing clothing in basements, attics, garages or anywhere else susceptible to moisture, sunlight, heat, grease and fumes. No closet space? Try a mobile garment rack. If you *must* store things in a less than ideal location, keep items off the floor and in properly enclosed containers. Use a dehumidifier if needed. Every few months, air out clothing and check its condition.

If you find a moth hole—Stop!

If there's a moth hole in a garment or you suspect an infestation in your closet, don't place the garment—or anything else from the closet—in out-of-season storage until you get rid of the existing pests. Use a safe insecticide and follow the directions on the label. Newer ones don't have a strong, penetrating smell and won't stain clothing when used properly. After eliminating an existing infestation, you can launder the clothes and store them back in the closet or in out-of-season storage with cedar or herbal protection.

One in, one out

Is it realistic to get rid of an old item every time you buy something new?

For some people, yes. For others, it's too much to think about on a regular basis. Your overall goal should be to maintain approximately the same size inventory in your closet. If it works for you to follow a "one in, one out" rule, then do so. But if you'd rather rebalance your wardrobe every six months or at the change of seasons, that's fine too.

Behind clothes doors

It's not uncommon to purchase a piece of clothing forget-
ting or not knowing that you have something very similar
in the far reaches of your closet. However, this can get
out of hand if your closet is really stuffed. An advertising
agency executive I worked with was stunned to discover,
as we emptied her closet and sorted her clothes by
category and color, that she had thirty-three black sweaters. She was disheartened to think of the money she had
spent on what were essentially duplicates of what she
already owned.

She chose to put a positive spin on the situation and donate most of the sweaters, as well as some other outfits
(all of which were in beautiful condition), to a charity sup-
porting women transitioning into the workforce. Once we
had her closet reorganized, it was much easier for her to
keep track of her inventory. She could find and wear what
she had instead of purchasing more.

4 Kitchen

Much of a family's time is spent in the kitchen. When the space is well organized, it's not only the hub of activity, it's also the heart of the home. It's a place to gather, share, talk and bond.

Take time now to clear the area of unnecessary items. Be objective about how many of the gadgets, containers and serving pieces collected over the years you actually use on a regular basis. Once you're decluttered, decide where you want to keep what's left. Place items where you can access them most efficiently based on the layout and traffic patterns in your kitchen.

Once your kitchen is streamlined, it will be easier to keep the kitchen clean, prepare wholesome meals and find time to spend together. It will be a space the whole family can enjoy.

Organize for healthy eating

The more organized your kitchen, the easier it is to eat well. To prepare healthy meals with minimal hassle, keep countertops clear and the pantry and refrigerator streamlined.

THE COUNTERTOPS

1. Store gadgets in drawers instead of on the counter.

2. Identify small appliances that are rarely used and place them elsewhere—either high up in a cabinet or on a shelf in the basement.

THE PANTRY AND THE REFRIGERATOR

1. Remove pantry contents and set them on the counter.

2. Group foods together by category (i.e., baking goods, snacks, pasta).

3. Toss anything expired. Combine "double items," like two half-empty boxes of the same cereal.

4. Wash the pantry shelves with soap and water or a disinfectant.

5. Reorganize contents within the pantry, labelling shelves if necessary.

6. Repeat steps 1-5 with what's in your fridge.

✳ Avoid piling personal papers and the kids' homework on the kitchen counters. These surfaces are for food. Establish a separate desk area (for your paper) and study center (for homework).

✳ **Use deep drawers** for bulky items such as pretzel and potato chip bags and loaves of bread. Large food storage containers can also go here. Shallow drawers are best for silverware, and everyday items such as dish towels and oven mitts.

✳ **In the cabinets,** use tiered plate racks to maximize stacking space. When storing mugs and cups, decrease the distance between shelves if possible, as space above them is often wasted. Increase the amount of stemware you can store on a shelf by turning every other glass upside down so they'll fit closer together.

✳ **Special shelving units** snap together around the pipes under the kitchen sink. Use them to create two levels of storage in this awkward area. Further maximize this space by attaching a holder for plastic wrap and foil to the inside of these cabinet doors.

One-motion storage

You should be able to reach ingredients, utensils, mixing bowls and serving dishes you use all the time without moving something else to get at what you want. This is known as one-motion storage. If your kitchen doesn't meet this test, rearrange it so your most frequently used items are at the front of the cabinets and gadgets are readily accessible in drawers.

If you want your kids to set the table, keep the plates and cups where they can reach them easily. While these items are traditionally stored in the upper cabinets, you can flip this arrangement and keep them in a cabinet below the countertop.

As one child clears the dinner dishes, have another set the table for breakfast. This will make the morning rush less stressful.

There's no match for this solution

Stow small food storage containers with the lids on. You'll save time hunting for a match. Yes, they take up more space this way, meaning you can store fewer pieces. But how many do you really need, considering you don't use them all at one time? Preventing the frustration and wasted time that accompanies searching for the right lid is worth it.

The next time you replenish your stock of food storage containers, purchase a set of ones that all use the same size lid. As long as some of the containers are deeper than others, you'll still have the ability to efficiently store a little or a lot. Finding the right lid, however, will be a lot faster.

Use heavy-duty resealable bags for long-term freezer storage. Squeeze out the extra air, flatten the bag, and food won't take up any more room than it has to. Use a permanent marker to note both the contents and the "eat by" date right on the bag.

A pet project

Your best friends (your dogs and cats) need to eat too. Create an area for their meals that's not in the path of kitchen traffic.

- Place food and water bowls on a vinyl placemat to protect your floor from water splashes and food spills.

- It makes sense to store the treats in this general area too. Devote one shelf of an upper cabinet to them.

- Keep a towel nearby for wiping muddy feet when pets come in through the back door.

- Transfer dry food bought in bulk to an airtight plastic container. If space is limited, keep a container that holds only a week's worth of food nearby and pour the rest into a larger container stored in a different location.

- Some homes have a drawer that's designed to hold food and water bowls at the right height for your pet. Pull it out to reveal the bowls, push it closed to make the kitchen look tidy. If you're not leaving bowls out on the floor, be sure your pet has access to fresh water on a regular basis.

Options for storing spices

ALPHABETIZING spices helps you find what you want at the grocery store; it will do the same at home. You're less likely to buy a duplicate of a spice you already have if your inventory is organized.

USE AN INDELIBLE PEN to write the purchase date on the bottle so out-of-date spices can be discarded. As a general rule, you can keep whole spices about two years but no longer than four years. Keep ground spices about one year but no longer than two years.

HEAT SOURCES can affect their quality, so don't store spices right by the stove, on top of the dishwasher or above the refrigerator. Keep them out of direct light and make sure their containers are airtight. Here are basic storage options:

STORAGE OPTIONS	TIPS ON ARRANGEMENT
In a cabinet.	Arrange them on a two-tiered turntable.
In a pantry.	Line them up on mini-steps, a freestanding unit that sits on a shelf and resembles stair steps.
In a drawer.	Use a specially-made insert that tilts up each row of spice jars.

Cook up a recipe solution

Make it easy to find your favorite recipes—and more likely that you'll actually try those enticing ones you've cut out of the newspaper.

- Highlight frequently used recipes in your cookbook's index so you can locate family favorites in a snap.

- Use plastic sleeves to protect your index card recipes from food stains, then organize them in a card box. The protective sleeves are available at kitchenware retailers.

- Convert a spare photo album into a personal cookbook by filling photo slots with clipped recipes.

- Or simply use a three-ring binder and staple loose recipes to blank paper. Tabbed dividers can be inserted in the binder to make it fast to flip to a category.

MENU PLANNING

Set aside half an hour on the weekend to decide what meals you'll serve the coming week. This is easier than you might think. Most families eat the same dishes on a rotating basis. You can work from a cheat sheet listing your family's favorite entrees and sides.

Master supermarket shopping

With this checklist strategy, grocery shopping will take less effort. You'll save the time it takes to handwrite a new list each week. You'll be less likely to forget to include an item on your list. And you can zip right through the store, never needing to backtrack to a previous aisle.

1. Type up a master grocery list reflecting everything you tend to purchase. Not sure what to include? Check your fridge and pantry to jog your memory. Leave a few blank spaces so you can write in specialty and one-time purchases.

2. Organize the list so the order of items corresponds to the arrangement of the aisles in your supermarket. (A trip to the store may be required to refine this.)

3. Make several copies and always keep one on the front of the refrigerator.

4. When you run out of something, circle it on your list. Likewise, as you plan upcoming meals, indicate needed ingredients on the list.

5. When you head for the store, simply grab your list.

Secrets of a clever coupon clipper

✳ **CLIP COUPONS** only for products you actually buy or have been meaning to try. Otherwise, you'll end up with so many that you'll be less likely to use the ones that are really pertinent to you.

✳ **ORGANIZE COUPONS** in an expandable accordion wallet that has prelabeled sections. When heading for the grocery, gather and paperclip needed ones together in the sequence the items appear on your list. If you need to check while shopping that you're putting the appropriate brand and size in your cart, it will be a cinch to find the right coupon.

Lunch to go

✳ Before putting extra food away after dinner, pack lunches using leftovers. This prevents having to pull everything out again in the morning.

✳ Keep unused plastic silverware from take-out dinners and put in a basket. You'll always have what you need for packing the kids' lunches.

✳ Buying individual serving size snacks can be expensive. To save money, buy snack foods in bulk and divide into mini resealable plastic bags. Keep a stock on hand for tossing into lunch bags.

Washing up

✳ Minimize the number of dirty dishes by using "3-in-1" containers—those that transfer safely from freezer to oven to table.

✳ Before cooking a large meal, fill a dishpan (or half the sink, if you have a divided one) with warm, soapy water. Drop in dirty utensils as you go and after dinner clean-up will be swift.

✳ Group together all forks, all spoons and all knives each in their own section of the dishwasher utensil basket. When it's time to put them away, simply grab all the utensils of one type and drop in the cutlery drawer. No sorting necessary.

✳ To unload the dishwasher efficiently, remove everything that belongs in a given cabinet before reaching for other dishes.

✳ Purchase a reversible clean/dirty magnet to place on the dishwasher so there's never a question about the status of what's inside.

✳ Keep it clean

Potentially messy surfaces stay clean with these quick tips:

- ✳ Wipe up a spill as soon as it occurs. Spend ten seconds now and you'll save minutes of scrubbing and scraping later.

- ✳ Place a baking sheet on the oven rack below pies and casseroles to catch drips and overruns. Apply these pans with non-stick cooking spray ahead of time so cleanup requires just a swipe.

- ✳ Place the clean lid of an empty margarine tub under metal cans, such as scouring powder, that are leaving rust stains in the cabinet.

- ✳ Do the same for sticky bottles such as those containing honey, syrup or cooking oil. Replace the lids with clean ones when they get too sticky.

Establish a kitchen telephone center

If supplies are handy, it's more likely that the family member answering your phone will take an accurate message.

1. Hang a small bulletin board (with plenty of thumbtacks) so there's a designated place for messages to be left.

2. Equip the area with phone directories, notepaper and a pen.

3. Attach the pen to the bulletin board with a piece of string. Tie the string to the pen, not the lid, otherwise the pen may "wander away."

The paper exchange

To track the school papers your kids need you to see, set up a desktop hanging file rack on the kitchen desk. Label one file folder with each child's name. Each afternoon, they can put school announcements and permission slips to be signed in there. You can check it in the evening and return necessary forms to their backpacks.

Periodically rearrange the papers posted on your refrigerator. If you have the same arrangement for too long, you become immune to the reminders that are posted there. How many times has a pizza-delivery coupon expired because you became so used to seeing it, you didn't see it anymore?

Is the side of your refrigerator your locale of choice for displaying children's artwork? Teach your children clutter control at a young age. Each week, let them choose a select amount of artwork to display. The rest can go elsewhere.

Staging to sell

When it's time to sell your house, before putting it on the market, take a day or two to "stage" the kitchen effectively. Prospective buyers want to see a large, inviting, uncluttered room. Here's how to give that impression, even if your kitchen is short on square footage:

1. Remove everything (including magnets, memos and photos) from the front and side of your refrigerator.

2. Clear the countertops of small appliances and personal or decorative items, leaving only the bare necessities.

3. Box up half of your dishes, glassware and mugs so the cabinets look spacious.

4. Clean everything thoroughly, including the inside of the oven, the pantry and the cabinets.

5. Top everything off by setting out a cookbook on a stand, a bowl of fresh fruit and maybe a small lamp for a warm glow.

 If you're willing to invest some money, a fresh coat of paint and new drawer handles and cabinet knobs will go a long way to updating your kitchen.

The dollars and sense of conquering kitchen clutter

Organizing your kitchen can save you money in many ways.

❋ Planning your menus a week at a time makes it more likely that you'll use ingredients already on hand rather than run to the store each evening for something new.

❋ In an organized pantry, everything is accessible so you don't buy duplicates of specialty foods you know you have but can't find.

❋ The same goes for what's in your cabinets. When pots, pans, dishes and utensils are in order, you don't forget about items used just once a year. You'll remember that Valentine's Day heart-shaped cake pan and won't need buy another.

❋ Shopping with a list makes you more inclined to purchase only what you need. You won't end up with impulse items bought in bulk that take up a lot of room but never get used up.

❋ When you can see what's in your refrigerator and freezer, you eat leftovers before they spoil and end up going to waste.

5 Time

You have two choices when it comes to use of time: what you do and how you do it. Choosing wisely about what you do makes you effective. Spending no more time than is necessary on a task makes you efficient. Both are important. If you begin your day with the most important item on your list, but it takes you three or four times longer to complete than it needs to because you can't find the right information in your files, you're effective, but not efficient. Conversely, if you spend all your time quickly completing tasks but they aren't ones that get you any closer to reaching one of your goals, what's the point? Just to cross as many items as possible off your list? In this instance, you're quite efficient, but not necessarily effective.

We all have the same twenty-four hours in each day, no more and no less. Making wise choices about how you spend what you have is one of the most important parts of being organized. It's when you're both effective and efficient that you have the greatest opportunity to live the life you want to live.

Many people feel compelled to participate in every opportunity that comes their way.

They also feel obligated to respond in the affirmative to every request for their volunteer service. But if you spread yourself too thin or you're not focused about how you use your time, you end up ignoring your own dreams and wishes. To make the best use of your time, reserve at least some of it for your personal interests and priorities instead of getting swept up completely in everything that everybody else wants you to do.

Saying "yes" and "no"

When your participation is requested and it doesn't fit with your new, focused life plan, say "no" graciously. Try this language: "I'm flattered you thought of me. I don't want to do your project a disservice by not giving it the full attention it deserves. My schedule is full at the moment. Thanks, though, for your confidence in me."

Of course, you also need to practice saying "yes." Feel awkward about accepting assistance? Consider saying: "Thanks, that would make this week easier on me. I hope you'll let me return the favor soon."

Sometimes you'll have to pass on things you'd *like* to do, but would send your life out of control if you did. Ask yourself, "Will this opportunity come around again? Do I want this enough now that I'm willing to be temporarily over-scheduled?" Sometimes you are, but that should be a conscious choice.

TO LESSEN TIME ON THE PHONE...

※ Dial just before lunch or right before dinner, when folks have meal planning on their minds and are hesitant to linger.

※ Set the stage for a brief conversation by beginning your call saying, "I just have a few minutes and want to tell you..."

※ Ask a rambling friend, "Is there anything else I can help you with now?" If she's just chatty, the answer will usually be "no" and you can then wrap up the call quickly.

For many people,

estimating how long it will take to finish a task or a project is the hardest part of managing their time. To make a reliable estimate, take your best guess as to how long a job will take. Then double that "best guess" and use the resulting figure when budgeting your time.

Why add so much time to your original calculation? To account for interruptions, stopping to get additional necessary information, and other distractions.

A REALISTIC TO-DO LIST has only as many tasks as you think will take you one-third of your time. One-third of the additional time will be accounted for by unexpected delays. The other third of your day will be occupied by new responsibilities that crop up as your day unfolds.

"The power of a list is not that it reminds you of what needs to be done, but that it frees you to forget."

Make your to-do list work for you.

1. **PUT EVERYTHING ON IT.** Do you worry you'll forget to look at your list, so you put other reminders on the back door or the mirror or around your computer screen? If you put everything on a single list, then this will be the *only* place you can find what needs to be done. So you won't forget to look there.

2. **MAKE EACH ENTRY SPECIFIC.** The action to be taken should be so clear that anyone reading your list could understand what needs to be done. With this as a guideline, you'll never have to figure out what you meant by an item.

3. **LIST ACHIEVABLE TASKS,** not the name of the entire project. Seeing a large undertaking on a daily list will be overwhelming and lead you to subconsciously bypass the item.

4. **COMPILE "NEXT STEPS."** As you complete each step on a project, note the next one. Using this technique, even the biggest jobs will eventually be completed.

✓ A list of lists

There are three basic types of lists. Using the right one at the right time can make your life easier.

MASTER LIST – Use this to capture random ideas floating around in your head. When you want to implement one of these ideas, work it into your task list.

TO-DO LIST – Best organized as a daily or weekly task list, this is most effective when it contains only what you think you can accomplish in that given window of time.

CHECKLIST – Create it once, use it forever. Examples include a master grocery list and a vacation or business travel packing template.

"Appointments" happen at a certain day and time.
"Tasks" can be performed at any point in time.

Due to this distinction, they need to be recorded in separate places. Appointments belong on your calendar; tasks on a list. This allows you to see at a glance where you *must* be on a given day, and what other time is *available* for you to tackle your tasks.

WHAT	WHEN	WHO	WHERE
Appointment.	Happens at set time.	Scheduled with someone,	Belongs on calendar.
Task.	Happens at any time.	Scheduled with yourself.	Belongs on list.

The exception? If you're consistently procrastinating on a task, one solution is to block out time on your calendar for it, creating an appointment with yourself.

At the beginning of each year, note all birthdays, school vacations and medical appointments on your new calendar. You'll be grateful you did all year long.

A plan is a roadmap...

designed to get you where you want to go.

It can be in the format of a promise to yourself about what you'll accomplish in the coming year, an outline of a home improvement project, or simply a to-do list for one day. It's best to write your plan down; this represents a commitment to yourself.

Once you subscribe to your plan, is it okay to deviate from it? Absolutely. If you're clear on what you had planned to do, when an unexpected opportunity presents itself you can weigh it against your intended path and evaluate whether the new option should take precedence.

For example, you may change your mind for financial reasons. You may have planned to redecorate your living room this month, but then discovered a limited-time sale on the kitchen cabinets you need. Or you may change your mind because the new opportunity is more personally fulfilling. Maybe you were going to do laundry, but then heard from a former neighbor who's visiting your city and wants to have lunch.

If you decide to change course, the fact that you have a plan means you know what you skipped over and you'll remember to come back to what you were doing.

Get past procrastination

There are many possible reasons for putting off until tomorrow what you intended to do today. It is only once you know *why you are doing it* that you can figure out *what to do about it.*

REASON	SOLUTION
You need more information to do the job right.	Replace what's currently on your list with a different task, such as "gather needed information."
It's overwhelming to think about.	Break the project down into smaller chunks. Don't post the project name on your list, only the next step.
The deadline is far away so you still have time.	Set interim deadlines to be sure the final one doesn't creep up on you.
You don't like the task.	Delegate it, swap with someone else, or create a reward system for yourself. Be sure to follow through on the reward, even if it's only a fifteen-minute break to read a magazine, or this technique will become less effective over time.
You don't know where to start.	Start anywhere. This will motivate you to continue and complete the task.
Other priorities get in the way.	Review your hopes and dreams. How important is this project to reaching them? Get clear on this so you know to move this item up the list or drop it permanently.

"How you use your time is your choice."

Have you ever been presented with a fantastic opportunity and said to yourself, "I don't have time to do that?" You do have time—the same amount as everyone else. Twenty-four hours each day. If you're not working an activity in, it's because you're using the time for something else. Instead of saying, "I don't have time to do that," try this more positive statement: "I choose to use my time in this other way."

Shape your day according to your energy levels.

Some tasks require innovative, creative thought. They are best addressed when your mind is sharp, when you're most alert. If you attempt them when you're tired, they will take twice as long to complete. Plus, the end result won't be as good. Reserve your low energy times for responsibilities that require no decision making and merely need to be performed.

HIGH-ENERGY TASKS	LOW-ENERGY TASKS
Writing thoughtful letters.	Filing papers.
Making important phone calls.	Doing dishes.
Goal planning.	Opening mail.
Talking with your child.	Paying bills.

Go from busy to productive

Suffer from how-fast-can-I-cross-off-my-list syndrome? It's common to be drawn to easy tasks and neglect the important (but more involved) items. You tell yourself you'll get to them "when you have time." You do have time, and this simple strategy will help you make the most of it.

1. Make your to-do list for today.

2. Include important tasks on which you've been procrastinating.

3. Number the entries on the list in the order in which you're going to do them.

Which task should be number 1? The easiest, to get the ball rolling? The hardest, to get it out of the way? Neither.

First should be the item that, if it were completed, would provide you the most value and move you that much closer to achieving your dream.

Actually numbering your list will make a world of difference. The numbers will guide you through your day and prevent both deviating to easy tasks and wasting time deciding what to do next.

The key to fitting in a major undertaking is to realize it's nothing but the sum of several small tasks.

Change your mind-set from "I have only fifteen minutes, I can't start anything," to "I have fifteen minutes, what one small piece of this project can I complete?"

If an endeavor seems long in duration, break it down in your mind. Instead of swimming thirty laps, think of it as swimming ten laps three times.

Waste no time

When a chore doesn't require your attention throughout, attack a second task before completing the first:

❊ Put in the laundry and then vacuum while waiting for the wash cycle to complete.

❊ Start the dishwasher and then file papers until it's time to put the dishes away.

Design simple shortcuts for common activities:

❊ Program your telephone's speed dial.

❊ Post a new master grocery list on the fridge after each shopping trip; circle items as you run out of them and your next list will be ready when you are.

❊ Provide two dirty laundry hampers so kids can separate darks from whites as they shed clothes—no need for you to re-sort later.

Look for routine tasks that can be done at the same time:

❊ Test your kids' spelling while cooking dinner.

❊ Work out and watch the news.

❊ Talk on the phone and fold laundry.

❊ Listen to educational or motivational information while commuting.

Your time is your own

I was presenting a workshop to a group of busy women and talking about time. I explained that it's never accurate to say, "I don't have time" because everyone has time. In fact, they have the same amount as everyone else. It's the great equalizer. A woman in the audience raised her hand in protest. Just that day, she had told a friend she didn't have time to meet her for coffee because she had to pick up her son from school. Her friend had more time available—enough time for coffee—but she simply didn't. I pointed out that she *did* have time for coffee, she was just *choosing* to use that time to pick up her son instead. I contended that she would never make the other choice because the consequence would be unacceptable (her son would be stranded), so she forgot it was even a choice.

Our conversation continued during the lunch break and she promised to think over what I had said. I asked her to let me know her conclusion. One month later, she reported back. She said that once she realized her schedule wasn't deter-mined for her, but was really a series of choices she made throughout the day, she felt much more in control of her life.

6 Storage

Smart storage means you can find what you want when you want it—and when it's time to put things back, you know where they go. When your possessions are stored well, they are protected from damage and your space looks clean and clutter-free.

Half the battle in getting organized is having the right tools. But arming yourself is *not* the first step. If you start at the store, you're likely to purchase containers based on eye appeal instead of true need.

Your best bet is to begin the organizing process in your home. Declutter each room and group similar items together. It's only after you know *what* you have and how *much* you have that you can make intelligent decisions about where you want to keep it and what new storage containers you might need.

Questions to ask before storing something

The less you have, the less you have to find a home for. But if you find it a challenge to part with anything, then asking yourself these questions may help:

- ✳ **Does this fall into the category of 'something important to me'?** It's not enough to surmise you "might need it someday." Keep only things that will move you closer to a goal.

- ✳ **Do I have the room to store this effectively?** Physical limitations must be considered.

- ✳ **If I wanted this later and didn't have it, how disappointed would I be?** If you think you could get over the feelings of regret quickly, it's worth the risk of pitching it.

- ✳ **If I had to replace this item later, how much would it cost?** If the outlay is negligible, it might be better to donate it, enjoy the clear space and purchase another when and if necessary.

- ✳ **Can I imagine a situation in which I would use this?** If not, then you probably don't need to keep it.

Container size is important. If a container is too large, you're likely to toss in unrelated items just because there's extra space. And if it's too small, of course not everything will fit.

✻

Are you prone to filling a tote to the brim? To keep the lid from popping off, select a brand where handles are attached to the container and pull up over the lid to latch it tightly in place.

✻

Look for storage tubs that stack securely. Choose ones designed so that the bottom of one container sits snugly on the lid of the one below.

Label liberally

It's faster to both find an item and put it away if
its storage spot—be it a shelf, a container or a file
folder—has a prominently placed label.

* Stacked boxes should be tagged on the side
  that faces outward, not the top, so contents
  can be identified without moving the boxes
  around.

* Label pantry shelves so when others put
  away groceries, the food actually ends up
  where it belongs.

* All electronic data backups that will be
  stored separately from the computer should
  have their contents noted on them immediately to avoid the hassle of having to use the
  computer to see what's on them.

* If you label the compartments in your junk
  drawer ("scissors," "tape"), you'll always
  know what's missing when one is empty.

When purchasing a handheld label-making device, be sure the tape it uses has a split back. With split-back tape, after you print out a label, all you have to do is bend it and the back will start to peel away from the adhesive label at the split. You'll avoid the annoyance of having to use your fingernail to try to separate a label from its backing.

Create compartments

Divide drawers into individual compartments. It's much easier to locate something if you have to look only in one small space than if you have to paw through the entire drawer.

✳ **MOLDED PLASTIC TRAYS** with multiple slots – These work well for office supplies, whether stored in the kitchen or home office. Similar trays that are fabric-lined can hold jewelry and help prevent it from getting scratched or tangled.

✳ **INDIVIDUAL TROUGHS** – You can find versions that hook together or ones that simply line up next to each other. Use them to keep lingerie drawers orderly so you can find the garment you need.

✳ **HONEYCOMB-STYLE DIVIDERS** – Sit one of these in a shallow drawer to create over thirty individual compartments. They're great for sorting socks, hosiery, ponytail scrunchies and other small items.

✳ **CUSTOM-CUT STRIPS** – These long plastic strips come in varied widths, from one to four inches. Determine how you want your drawer divided, cut lengths of the strips to match your design and secure them in the drawer using accompanying adhesive connectors. This customizable system is ideal for kitchen gadgets, which come in all shapes and sizes.

"While many people may need better storage, they don't usually need more storage.

They just need less stuff."

✳ Even stuff you like and intend to keep can become clutter if it's in the wrong place. If you can't find something you know you have, then it's of no use to you.

✳ Stash often-used belongings near where you'll need them, not "where they fit," and they'll be easier to get to when you want them.

✳ If you use an object infrequently and are afraid you won't remember later where it is, ask yourself, "If I were searching for this today, where would I think to look for it?" Then store it there.

Think vertical

If you're short on space, create additional storage by maximizing use of vertical space.

- ❉ Use one tall file cabinet instead of two short ones.

- ❉ Put a hutch over your home office desk.

- ❉ Install floor-to-ceiling shelves on an empty wall.

If you store a lot up high, keep a folding step stool handy. When it's not in use, stash it between the refrigerator and the wall or in the back of the coat closet.

Double-duty furniture

Get twice the value from furniture that both serves a function and has additional storage space.

❋ **WOODEN FILE CABINETS** make cute end tables.

❋ **AN ANTIQUE TRUNK** can store blankets and throws and create extra seating in your living room.

❋ **A COFFEE TABLE** with a shelf underneath accommodates unread magazines and newspapers.

❋ **A TRUNDLE BED** with the mattress removed can serve as a toy chest.

❋ **CERTAIN STEP STOOLS** open to reveal a toolbox.

❋ **A STORAGE BENCH** can hold mittens and hats while also providing a place to sit down and put on boots and shoes.

Create an eye-catching spot

to stash outgoing items: clothes headed for the dry cleaners, packages to mail, library books to be returned. Choose a location that you pass on the way out the door so you'll always remember to check it. There will be no more I-wish-I-had-that-with-me when you're out running errands.

Make a mudroom

If you don't have a mudroom, fashion a comparable space in your back hall or near the door to the garage.

A bench paired with hooks or cubbies on the wall will do; if you want to splurge, a locker for each child is even better. Kids can leave backpacks, coats, hats and gloves here when they come home from school. If the space is in or near the laundry area, they can shed muddy clothes as they return from sports activities and drop them right into a hamper.

Looking for a place to keep extra inventory?

Putting objects inside empty luggage is often an ideal solution. After all, the suitcases are already taking up space in your attic or basement. You might as well fill them up. Good candidates for such storage are the extra pillows, blankets and towels that you haul out only for out-of-town company.

Big and bulky storage

IF YOU DON'T HAVE STORAGE BOXES or other options available for bulky items such as bed pillows, comforters and down-filled winter jackets, place them in bags. Extra large, see-through, resealable plastic bags (ones that are as large as trash bags) will protect your possessions from dust, dirt and water.

TO STORE MORE IN LESS ROOM, use a vacuum-seal bag. Pack up to the fill line, seal and use your vacuum cleaner to suck out all the air through the bag's special valve. The package will shrink in size remarkably. When you next open it, the items inside will expand back to their original size.

Special treasures include a grandmother's wedding dress, a collection of sports memorabilia and a child's first creative writing.

If you want to preserve these for posterity, seek specific information on the appropriate storage methods. They must be protected from the most common causes of damage and deterioration, including:

- Handling and use.

- Exposure to light.

- Extreme temperature and humidity.

- Water.

- Insects.

- Pollutants.

Pare down before adding on

A family that hired me for a consultation shared that they felt overrun with toys, furniture, household items and clothing. As part of our conversation, we talked about the benefits of paring down, including how much money they might be able to recoup (by donating some of the excess) or save (by changing their future purchase patterns).

It was then that they revealed that before calling me, they had put an addition onto their home to hold the clutter. My advice may not come cheap, but it usually costs less than adding on to a house! Judging by how much clutter they decided to part with, we could have saved them the cost of the remodel.

My recommendation to anyone convinced that they need more storage space is to seriously consider purging possessions first. It will be less hassle and, even if you hire professional help, it will be less expensive than renting a storage unit, moving to a bigger apartment or adding on to your house.

7 Home Office

A home office can be used for running a business or for the business of running a family. Either way, there is money coming in, money going out, a schedule to be maintained and information to be stored. Whether you dedicate an entire room to this function or carve out a portion of another room to serve as your command central, it's important to have definitive work and storage spaces. This allows you to both find and put away information quickly and to get down to business when you need to.

When your home office is well-organized, it's a welcoming space in which to work. If you enjoy being there, you're more likely to keep up with daily responsibilities. And with good systems in place, you can minimize time spent on administrative tasks and stay on top of the finances, saving or making more money for your family.

Location, location, location

If you are fortunate enough to have a spare room to call your own, take advantage of it. You can set up your office exactly as you want it to be. But not everyone has this option. If you're choosing from other spaces, here are points to keep in mind.

LOCATION	PROS	WHAT TO KNOW
GUEST ROOM	Unless you have constant visitors, most of the time the space will serve exclusively as an office.	Opt for closed storage options, such as bookcases with doors or armoires. Your "office life" will be out of sight when you have visitors. Purchase a sleeper sofa instead of a regular bed to save on space.
KITCHEN	You already spend a lot of time in this room, so files and paperwork will be convenient if kept here.	Avoid using the kitchen table as your desk. Clearing your papers away each evening to set the table is not productive. File cabinet space is limited here, so designate another area of the home for long-term file storage.
LIVING ROOM	This is usually one of a house's larger rooms, so you have space to spread out.	Use a freestanding screen or tall plants to section off the area serving as your office. Your work won't stare you in the face during family time. If a computer is kept here, all family members will want to use it.

Is this space right for a home office?

Ask yourself these questions when deciding if an area will work as your office:

- ❋ Is there enough room to accommodate my needs?

- ❋ Is the wiring adequate?

- ❋ Am I far enough away from other family members that I won't be disturbed?

- ❋ Am I close enough to other family members that I'm accessible if needed?

- ❋ Will I be able to separate my office work from the rest of my life?

- ❋ Will I enjoy spending time there?

 If you work from home, are you often distracted by the sight of chores that need to be done? Try turning off the lights in every room but your office, or closing doors to other rooms.

"Having physical space to spread out gives you mental space to think and create."

Many people underestimate the value of having clear desk space. But how many times have you spread an important project out on the dining room table (at home) or an empty conference table (at work) so you can focus better?

Imagine finding such room to work *right at your desk*. You can if you use an L-shaped desk, because this configuration provides one area on which to arrange project files and another on which to do actual work. To use the space effectively:

1. Organize the projects you intend to tackle that day on one leg of the L—the "layout area."

2. Spread out the first project you want to address on the other leg of the L—the "work surface."

3. When you need to switch between projects, gather up the papers you're currently working on and square them into a pile.

4. Set that pile on the layout area. Pick up the next item needing your attention.

5. Turn back to the work surface, spread out these papers, and begin to work.

Home office basics

In addition to a desk and a chair, gather these fundamentals to make your home office space both functional and comfortable:

- ❋ Inbox for containing unread mail.

- ❋ Outbox for items to be mailed or passed on to someone else.

- ❋ Desktop file rack to hold current project files.

- ❋ File cabinet for less frequently accessed information.

- ❋ Computer, printer and other needed electronics.

- ❋ Wastepaper basket, recycling bin or shredder for discarding junk mail and unnecessary paper.

- ❋ Drawer organizers to keep supplies sorted.

- ❋ Clock that is easily visible from all areas.

- ❋ Decorative items such as photos, artwork and live plants to personalize the space.

Daily, Weekly, Monthly

For the most efficient setup, arrange your home office using daily-weekly-monthly criteria.

✳ **DAILY.** Supplies you use every day should be within arm's reach when you're sitting at your desk.

✳ **WEEKLY.** Inventory and information you access only now and then can be on the other side of the room.

✳ **MONTHLY.** If your office space is limited and you need an item less than once a month, store it in a different room or even offsite.

Think of your desktop as prime real estate available only to your most valuable properties. Review the supplies that have taken up permanent residence there. Should some of them be moved to another home?

Small space extenders

When your home office is small, make use of the vertical space in the room. Both furniture plans and desktop arrangements can help with this.

* Tall bookcases work well for storage or display. Adjustable shelves allow you to maximize space; move them closer together when the shelf holds only short items.

* A hutch extending above your desk makes excellent use of wall space. Use it to house frequently accessed books and keep cumbersome supplies off your desktop.

* Instead of two 2-drawer file cabinets, consider one 4-drawer unit. You can file twice as much information without taking up any more floor space.

* Mount the base unit of your portable phone to the wall. Also use a wall clock instead of a desktop version. This strategy will free up precious desk space.

* Tilt your planner or calendar up on your desk by placing it on a small easel or a cookbook stand. It will be easy to view your schedule a glance, the planner won't become buried under paper, and the total footprint it occupies on your desk will be smaller.

* Space-saving tools, such as a stapler that stands up on end, save both desk space and time. With one motion, you can pick it up and staple a document—no fumbling to get your hand into the right position.

A MASTER FAMILY CALENDAR hung on the wall in a central location (perhaps by your desk in the kitchen) is a time-tested solution for when multiple people have to keep track of several other people's schedules. Parents can list trips and work schedules, particularly if their shifts vary. Children can record data about sports practices and extra-curricular activities.

For most families, the month-at-a-glance calendar format works fine. This provides enough room to list events while still permitting everyone to see the "big picture" of what's coming up. The information can be handwritten or entered into a computer program and then printed out and posted.

You can also keep a personal planner. Use it to track the details of your daily plans. But other than the master family calendar and this, don't record appointments and tasks in any other place. If you have to check several sources for notes, you waste time and increase the chance that you'll overlook a reminder.

Reading pile unrealistic?

With so much information available, it's not uncommon to feel overwhelmed at the thought of reading it all. Try these strategies to shrink your reading list.

- ❋ Ask yourself if you're reading something because you will enjoy it and/or it will benefit you in some way. If not, reprioritize your reading pile and see what can be eliminated.

- ❋ Set aside one hour twice a week as reading time. If you stick to this, you'll be amazed at how much you can get through.

- ❋ If you commute to work on public transportation or often have waiting time between appointments, create a mobile reading file. Stash interesting articles in a folder secured with a clasp and keep it with you.

- ❋ If you prefer not to rip apart your magazines, use a highlighting marker to identify in the table of contents which articles you want to read. Each time you grab the journal, you can pick up where you left off without wasting time deciding what's of interest.

Subscribe to this idea

Saving old magazines for their seasonal ideas? Instead of shelving them in strict chronological order, organize them by month. For example, keep all of the December issues of your home décor magazines together. When you need a clever holiday decorating idea, simply head for the December shelf and browse.

PASS IT ON. Some people feel both less wasteful and more thrifty if they pass magazines on to a friend because it makes their investment go further. If that describes you, place publications in a basket by the door until you're scheduled to see your friend.

Check bill paying off your list

Bill paying is a monthly routine for everyone. Set up a streamlined system to shrink the amount of time it takes and reduce the chance that you'll get behind and incur late fees and interest charges.

PAPER BILLS

If you receive bills in the mail and pay them by check, designate one place in the house for unpaid invoices to avoid losing them. To be most efficient:

1. As you open bills, check the charges. If you need to dispute an amount, you'll want to do it as soon as possible.

2. Remove advertisements and bill stuffers and toss them if they're of no interest to you. Place the bill and reply envelope back in the original mailing envelope.

3. If you pay bills twice a month, organize them in a desktop sorter with two slots. File invoices that you routinely pay on the first of the month in the front slot. Put statements that you intend to pay on the fifteenth in the back slot.

4. If you prefer to maximize your money, sending payments just before the due date, organize bills in the order they'll need to be paid.

5. When you're ready to pay bills, simply grab what's up next. You'll avoid having to sort through to find ones that are due.

ONLINE BILLS

Receiving and paying bills online saves hours. It also gives you a lot of control over your finances; not only can you schedule the payment time and amount, but online account monitoring is a fast way to detect fraud. Here's how to work with online bill paying:

1. You can receive an e-mail reminder when a bill is due, or simply log on periodically to the website where you're set up to receive and pay bills electronically. (Usually this is your bank's website.)

2. Review the electronic bills (e-bills) that have been delivered to your online account.

3. For each bill, designate the payment amount and select the date you'd like it paid. You can do this in advance, scheduling the system to make payments later in the month.

4. To save even more time, consider setting up automatic payment on recurring bills. To avoid unpleasant surprises, you can arrange that bills are paid only if the total is under a certain amount. If anything exceeds that amount, you will receive notification. (This is a great way to keep an eye on your energy bill.)

5. You can also use online bill paying to pay vendors or individuals who don't (or can't) accept electronic payment. The system will mail a hardcopy check for you.

Document important information

There is a lot of essential information to keep track of when running a household. Take time to transcribe instructions and schedules that are only "in your head" so that you and others have it at your fingertips.

* Compose a "How to Run the House" manual. Include seasonal maintenance schedules, appliance instructions and emergency procedures. Keep printouts of all these documents in a neon-colored binder that is highly visible.

* Establish a file for product manuals. Staple receipts for major purchases to the first page of the instructions. Note the warranty expiration date right on the sales slip.

* Create a babysitter instruction sheet. Include information about your house (full address, phone number), children (ages, weights, allergies, medications), routines (bedtime, TV rules, snacks), where you'll be (including full contact information), and alternate contacts (neighbors, grandparents). Type in information that is constant. Leave blanks to handwrite details that will change.

REAL-LIFE SECRET

My first office

When I first became an entrepreneur, I was young, single and living in a one-bedroom apartment. The living room had a divided layout and I was able to fashion an office out of half of it. However, the only phone jack was in the bedroom. Every time the phone rang, I had to go into the bedroom to answer it. (This was in the days before cordless phones or e-mail.)

No problem, I thought (naively). The bedroom wasn't that far away. And I answered the phone professionally so no one calling thought anything other than they were calling my office.

I mentioned this casually to a business consultant I had hired. She wasted absolutely no time telling me to get a phone jack installed at my desk. "Really?" I asked. I wondered if it could possibly be worth the expense at this early stage of my business. Nonetheless, I heeded the advice.

What an unbelievable difference! It wasn't just the time savings (not having to go into the other room) or the comfort (sitting at my desk, not on my bed). It was the atmosphere. It was the energy that came from taking myself seriously and treating my space accordingly. My business grew rapidly. From that moment, I have never, ever doubted the value of a well-designed, well-organized workspace.

8 Bed & Bath

Your bedroom and bathroom are private spaces in your home. However, just because others don't see them regularly doesn't mean it's okay to neglect them. In a sense, they're even more important to organize well because they're the first places you see in the morning and the last you see at night.

Fortunately, once you're got them in order, it's easy to maintain these spaces. A few simple actions (making the bed, putting away clothes, hanging up towels) go a long way in keeping rooms appealing.

If kept clutter-free, the bedroom and the bathroom are restful havens from the hustle and bustle of the rest of the world. When they're orderly, you can begin and end your day in peace.

Time how long your morning routine takes to complete. Once you know this statistic, simply count backwards from your anticipated departure time to see when you must get up on any given day.

※

Instead of stressing about what time you have to rise, focus on what time you need to go to bed to wake up naturally at the appointed hour. As long as you go to bed on time, getting up should be relatively easy.

※

Buy a clock for the bathroom. It's where most people lose time in the morning, whether it's lingering in a long shower or taking extra time to do their hair. Keep an eye on the time to stay focused and efficient.

YOUR BEDSIDE TABLE or nightstand should not be much taller than the top of the mattress so that you can reach items easily from the bed. Place your clock, lamp and the book you're currently reading on top; use the drawer to hold less attractive items such as contact lens solution and hand cream tubes.

LITTLE EFFORT, BIG DIFFERENCE

Always make your bed

It has the biggest impact on how organized your bedroom looks. Plus, it's a task that requires little thought so it's fast and easy to do.

POCKETS OFTEN GET EMPTIED ONTO THE TOP OF THE DRESSER.

Keep the miscellany organized

with a dresser top valet—a shallow tray divided into sections for holding keys, cash, business cards, employee badges, rings, watch and anything else you'll need again the next morning.

Coin-sorting tubes or a battery-operated sorting machine, available at drugstores or gift retailers, also come in handy on the dresser. Utilize them to organize all those loose coins so they can be exchanged for bills at the bank. Spare change adds up to a lot.

Hidden labels

Labels on the outside of dresser drawers aren't attractive. Instead, open each drawer and place a label identifying its contents on the top, flat surface of the drawer front. It will be visible whenever the drawer is opened. Being reminded in this way about what belongs in a drawer makes it less likely that someone will toss in a garment that doesn't belong.

Use deep dresser drawers for bulky items like sweatshirts and jeans. Reserve shallow drawers for items that take up less space, such as socks and lingerie. Use drawer organizers of different shapes and sizes to keep the small items in order.

KEEP A DIRTY LAUNDRY HAMPER IN EACH BEDROOM.
When hampers are conveniently located, family members are less
likely to drop dirty clothes on the floor. (Use a divided version or
place two of them side-by-side if you want whites and darks to be
separated at this stage of the laundry process.)

**ENSURE AN ADEQUATE SUPPLY OF HANGERS IN EACH
CLOTHING CLOSET.** When time-pressed individuals have empty
hangers at their fingertips, they're more likely to hang up clothing
that is clean or can be worn again. Otherwise it's often tossed
over the back of a chair.

A hook on the back of the closet door is a great
place to hang the next day's outfit. Planning
ahead allows you to double-check that the clothes
you intend to wear are clean and pressed.

Organization is within your child's reach

When organizing a child's bedroom, accessibility to toys and supplies should be your number-one priority. Storage containers should be:

- ❋ Low enough for them to reach.

- ❋ Easy for them to get into.

- ❋ Clearly identified as to what belongs in them.

❋ Avoid using weighty toy chests or window seats that lift to reveal storage underneath. A child can get trapped inside them, or a heavy lid can hit them on the head or squash their fingers.

Put it up

Belongings that your child doesn't handle regularly (like sports trophies and beloved, but outgrown stuffed animals) can be stored in a less accessible area of the bedroom. Install a shelf high up on a wall, just a few feet below the ceiling. Choose a wall other than the one behind the bed so nothing is hanging over him while he sleeps. Arrange prized possessions artfully and the display will be as decorative as the wallpaper border you would normally find in this spot.

✳ This is mine, that's yours

Color coding kid items can cut down on bathroom bickering about who has claim to what.

1. Assign one colored towel and washcloth to each child, or let each child choose his or her own color. No one will be able to reasonably declare a sibling used his.

2. Carry the theme through to toothbrushes and water cups.

3. Stack small plastic drawers on the bathroom counter to hold their other items, like floss and adhesive bandages. Use a colored sticker to flag which drawer belongs to which child.

Clean up the bath toys

When you have young children, toy clutter spills over into the bathroom. Keep playthings out of the way after bath time with one of these options:

❋ A toy basket that attaches to the tile wall with suction cups.

❋ A mesh bag that hooks over the shower nozzle.

❋ A plastic step-stool that opens to reveal additional storage.

Bathroom storage

The bathroom is one of the smallest rooms in the house, yet it's used for multiple activities, like bathing, grooming and dressing. Organize for easy access to all that's stored here.

> ❋ Group products according to how they're used: showering, shaving, makeup application and removal, and hair styling. Each collection belongs in its own container.

> ❋ Utilize the space under a pretty pedestal sink by stacking equally attractive woven baskets there. Coordinate with a waste basket of similar material.

> ❋ Purchase a freestanding unit that straddles the toilet tank and has open shelves or a closed cabinet above. This is an excellent place to store extra toilet paper.

> ❋ If you have available floor space, bring in furniture from other rooms to create additional storage. Would the pretty night-stand you're replacing as you redecorate your child's bedroom become a perfect towel cabinet?

> ❋ Look to the back of the door for another storage opportunity. A multi-pocket organizer hung here can hold a curling iron, hairdryer, brushes and aerosol cans.

Have one set of cleaning products stored in each bathroom

so it's convenient to disinfect at any point in time. Store on a high shelf or in a cabinet with a child safety lock if there are youngsters in the house.

Keep a roll of paper towels or a rag in each bathroom so you can quickly mop up water on the sink, counter or floor.

Shop for all-purpose cleansers that can clean multiple surfaces. You'll find you can actually get by with fewer products.

Make over your makeup

Bottles, tubes, jars... beauty product clutter is common. Clear out what's old and separate the rest as detailed below. It will be faster to put your best face forward each morning.

1. Review all your cosmetics and toss out expired ones. When you're not sure about a product, see if it has an expiration date on it (many do) or get advice from your department store cosmetics counter.

2. Place makeup you use daily in a basket that sits on your vanity or dressing table. It's faster to sweep it all into one open container after using it than to spend time slotting each product into a multi-partitioned organizer.

3. Identify items you know you'll never use. As long as they're recent and unopened, put them aside to donate to a women's charity.

4. Slip sample-size makeup into a zippered pouch and place in a drawer. Take these space-saving versions on trips instead of the full-size ones you use at home.

5. Reserve little bottles of hotel shampoo and lotion for your out-of-town guests' convenience. Keep them in your guest bedroom.

6. Be mindful of future clutter accumulation traps—department store promotions, hotel toiletry freebies, impulse purchases. The next time you're tempted to add to your collection, remember how much space they took to store and how much time it took you to clean them out.

GROUP TOWELS in your linen closet according to the bathroom in which they go. Store large beach towels on a high shelf during the off season. Retire worn towels to the garage for greasy, muddy jobs.

ORGANIZE SHEETS BY SIZE: twin, full, queen or king. Label sections of your linen closet shelves and place sets appropriately. For quick retrieval, fold a complete set of sheets and place inside one of the pillowcases; you'll never have to search for missing pieces again. Don't have a linen closet? Store clean sheets and towels in the bedroom or bathroom in which you use them.

3 options for wrinkle-free storage

There are ways to store freshly washed and ironed table linens so they remain relatively wrinkle-free:

1. Drape over a rod in your linen closet.

2. Fold lengthways a few times and store on a pants hanger.

3. Roll around empty wrapping paper tubes and fasten tightly with a straight pin.

9 Garage, Attic & Basement

In many homes, the garage, attic and basement have long been neglected when it comes to organizing. Guests don't see these areas. You may not see them every day—out of sight, out of mind.

These rooms are important to organize, however, if for no other reason than you have so much stored there. If you can quickly find something (or remember that you have "one of those" in the first place), you not only save time, you also save the money you'd spend buying a replacement for a missing item.

Though it may not seem like it on the surface, getting these spaces in order can also motivate you to pursue your personal goals. If you find the family history documents you need to begin your genealogy project or you create a space to do the woodworking you love, this may be just the boost you need to get going.

It pays to pay attention

Once you realize how much it can pay to pay attention to these neglected spaces, you may be more inclined to spend some time organizing them. For example:

❊ When it's obvious where tools and equipment belong in the garage, it's easier to put them away at the end of the day, making it less likely they will be left outside. How much could you save by not having to replace rusted garden tools and ruined yard equipment?

❊ The attic is often home to holiday decorations. But how many times have you not fully decorated your house because it was just too much trouble to find everything and bring it down? Wouldn't you prefer to get your money's worth out of all the decorations you've bought?

❊ The basement is a fine area for an exercise room—if you have enough space for the equipment. Want to get that treadmill or clothes rack out of your bedroom? What if clearing away some basement clutter was all the incentive you needed to do this and get started with a fitness program?

WHEN TO USE EACH SPACE

The garage, attic and basement are often thought of in the same way: places to stash items you don't know what else to do with. While all three can serve as storage spaces, each is unique and should be used in a different way.

✳︎ **Garage.** Use the garage to hold equipment that's used outdoors or is usually dirty. If you have items too large to store in the house, such as off-season patio furniture, it can go here. It's also appropriate to set up an area for belongings you take with you when leaving the house, such as gloves, hats and scarves.

✳︎ **Attic.** In many homes, this space is hard to get to. Reserve it for items you won't need for a while, such as dishes you'll hand down when your child goes off to college. While neither of these three spaces is a good choice for delicate items such as vintage books, the temperatures in an attic can be the most extreme and potentially damaging.

✳︎ **Basement.** The basement is the most likely of the three spaces to have some measure of climate control; you can enhance this by using a dehumidifier. It's a comfortable place for work centers such as laundry, exercise or crafting spaces. If you absolutely don't have room for storing out-of-season clothes in the main part of your house, this is the next best choice, especially if all or part of your basement is finished.

Clutter accumulates in the far corners of

garages, attics and basements. Before you reorganize and reorder what is stored in these rooms, clear out what you no longer need. Prompt yourself to get rid of as much as possible with these questions:

✳ **DO WE USE THIS REGULARLY?** If you find sports gear your children have outgrown or exercise equipment you no longer use, consider consigning it at a resale shop or having a garage sale.

✳ **IS IT STILL FUNCTIONAL?** Lawn equipment that doesn't work should be repaired or discarded.

✳ **DO I KNOW WHAT THIS IS?** Extra parts that can't be identified may be left over from a project completed years ago. Do you really need to keep them if you don't know what they're for?

✳ The attic, basement and garage aren't ideal storage spaces, especially for some items. Temperature and humidity fluctuate widely in these spaces, and water leaks are possible. Because of this, don't store financial or sentimental valuables in these areas, including: family history photos, negatives, videotapes, CDs, DVDs and other computer media; paper products such as books, scrapbooks, newspaper clippings; heirloom clothing including christening gowns and wedding dresses; and antique furniture.

Use vertical space in the garage

The garage, which is meant to protect your cars, often houses everything *but* the vehicles. Why? Because the floor space is already occupied. Make room for the cars while still storing seasonal and activity-based equipment by taking advantage of all the wall space. Use a combination of hooks, shelves, bins and baskets, and cabinets—either freestanding units or a wall-mounted system.

✳ **Hooks** are effective for storing long-handled tools, such as rakes, hoes and shovels. Use them to hold coiled hoses and extension cords. Suspend your ladders horizontally on a series of hooks.

✳ **Shelves** work well for grouping related items such as flowerpots, gloves and gardening clogs. Reserve lower shelves for heavy items such as bags of potting soil or mulch.

✳ **Bins and baskets** are recommended for holding multiples of the same item. Use medium-sized ones for different kinds of tape and string, small ones to sort nails and screws.

✳ **Cabinets** that are locked are the best place in the garage to store chemical products. Behind closed doors they won't catch a child's inquiring eye; behind locked doors they're inaccessible.

Children who play multiple sports accumulate a lot of gear.

LARGE, STACKABLE, CLEAR PLASTIC DRAWERS are great for organizing and holding it all. Position a set strategically in the garage along the wall that's between the car and the door to the house. Label each according to the sport and contents (example: "Soccer—cleats and shin guards"). Get the kids in the habit of dropping their gear in the appropriate drawer as they return home from each practice or game.

BICYCLES don't have to be parked on the floor. You can elevate them with a wall-mounted storage rack (holds one bike), a gravity rack that stands near the wall but is not attached to it (holds up to two bikes) and a tension pole anchored between the ceiling and floor with hooks extending from both sides (holds up to four bikes).

Is your garage littered with soccer balls, footballs and basketballs? Corral them into a large, clean trash can or a large hammock-type net attached to the wall.

Nail this

There are multiple options for storing tools. Choose an option based on your preferences and needs.

✳ **VISIBLE** – If you do most of your tinkering at a garage workbench, you'll want your tools to be visible and within reach. Hand tools, such as hammers, screwdrivers and wrenches, can be hung from a pegboard or grid system that is attached to the wall above your workspace.

✳ **HIDDEN** – Some people feel more organized with everything put away. If you're one of them, use a tool cabinet with multiple drawers. This also works well for tools that are too heavy to hang on the wall. Tools that come in a hard-sided case can be stored in that case. Any attachments that also came in the case will be right with the tool when you need them.

✳ **PORTABLE** – If your work takes you to multiple locations, opt for a portable solution. Choices include a standard tool box, a dual purpose step-stool that opens to reveal tool storage space and a tool bucket that has storage pockets around the outside and space inside for large items like extension cords.

Attic storage

Attics are frequently the least convenient storage space in the house. Many are accessed only through a pull-down staircase or a hole in the ceiling. Reserve your attic space for items you need only a few times per year or less, including holiday décor or toys and furniture you're saving for the next baby.

✳ Holiday decorations should be in plastic totes with lids securely attached. Label containers on the side that faces forward so you can tell what's in each without unstacking them. Don't put candles in the attic over the summer because they can melt in the heat.

✳ Cover furniture with a sheet to protect it from dust and dirt. If you have reason to fear water leaks from the roof, use a plastic tarp instead. Valuable antiques should be stored elsewhere; perhaps you can incorporate your grandmother's treasures into your everyday furnishings.

✳ Lay flat items such as extra shutters, tent poles or skis where the roof slants down to meet the floor.

✳ Are you keeping luggage and trunks up here? There's additional, often-neglected room inside all of these. Use them to hold extra blankets and pillows or place small suitcases inside larger ones.

Create a floor where there isn't one

If your attic doesn't have a finished floor but instead has exposed floor joists, your storage opportunities are limited because there's nowhere to set your belongings. Change this by using plastic panels designed specifically to create a floor surface in unfinished attic spaces. Installation is quick and easy; follow the manufacturer's directions. Alternatively, you can have a contractor create a wooden floor for you.

The next time you are hauling boxes up to the attic, ask yourself if you're doing so just to avoid making a decision about what to do with what's inside. If the answer is yes, resolve to decide now rather than postpone a decision for months or years. Resist the temptation to stash boxes of "miscellaneous stuff" up there. Chances are you would just forget about them until your next move.

Laundry center

Laundry is ongoing. By equipping your laundry center and streamlining your routine, and this task won't take any longer than it has to.

- Cut down on sorting time by having family members divide their own clothes between two dirty-clothes hampers. Children who are old enough to put clothes in a hamper are capable of separating whites from darks.

- Keep a stain removal product nearby so spots can be treated immediately, before they set and become time-consuming to remove.

- Affix a magnetic caddy to the side of the washer to hold coins and other objects found in pockets.

- Keep a pin-cushion with threaded needles on hand. Repair loose buttons before washing the garment so they aren't lost in the wash.

- Purchase inflatable hangers so you can drip-dry select garments without ruining their shape.

- Hang shirts that need ironing as soon as you unload the dryer. Tossing them in a basket only causes more wrinkles to iron.

- Fold towels before the other clean laundry. Once their bulk is removed from the basket, the rest will appear more manageable.

- Have the kids match up clean socks while they watch TV.

In many houses, the door to the basement is in the kitchen or nearby. This makes the basement a convenient place to store small appliances you don't use often as well as extra canned goods that don't fit in the pantry. Place a set of shelves at the bottom of the basement stairs to hold this overflow. This is also a good place to keep your extra stock of paper towels and toilet paper.

✳

The door to the basement or garage represents another storage option. Items that absolutely don't fit in your kitchen but must be kept close by can be placed in a rack attached to the back of the basement door. Non-food items can be placed in a rack on the door to the garage.

SET ASIDE A SPOT IN YOUR BASEMENT to store the original packaging for expensive products that are under warranty. If you need to return an item, this packaging may be required. Even if it's not, having the original box and internal padding makes it easy to mail if necessary. If your credit card extends your manufacturer's warranty, the total amount of time to retain these boxes will be extended. Stick a note on the box with the date the warranty expires so you'll know when you can recycle it.

MANY PEOPLE KEEP CARDBOARD BOXES to use when mailing packages and gifts. This is fine as long as you store only as many as you will reasonably use in the next twelve months. Collapse them flat so they take up less room. If there's a risk of water on the floor, elevate them by placing bricks underneath. Remember: once you have enough boxes, you don't need to keep new ones that come in the mail.

Garage sale success secrets

To hold a profitable garage sale, two things need to happen: People have to show up and they need to buy. Here are strategies that successful sellers use:

1. Advertise in your local newspaper. List specific items; often it's the lure of particular furniture pieces, collectibles or toys that attracts buyers.

2. Post large, legible signs where allowed in your neighborhood. At intersections, add an arrow so drivers know where to turn.

3. Price everything ahead of time. Most people will bargain but they need a starting point. And shy buyers will often leave empty-handed rather than ask the cost.

4. Put names on unusual items so it's clear what they are.

5. Place items along the driveway so people can move around. Station large pieces near the sidewalk to attract attention.

6. If you must display goods in the garage, brighten the space with lamps from your house (clearly mark them as not-for-sale).

7. Use card tables and clothing racks to showcase merchandise. No one likes to dig through items jumbled in a cardboard box on the floor.

8. Have an extension cord handy so buyers can test electronics. Provide a mirror if you plan to sell clothing.

9. Recruit a friend to be your cashier so you're free to mingle. Have plenty of coins and small bills on hand for making change.

IS A GARAGE SALE YOUR BEST OPTION?

The thought of receiving cash for items you no longer want is appealing. However, sometimes items sell for very little (or not at all) at a garage sale. You may benefit more by donating items to a non-profit organization and claiming a tax deduction (check with your tax advisor) or selling on an online auction site. Given the additional fact that holding a garage sale takes time, the donation or online options are worth considering. Of course, if you enjoy setting up garage sales, then by all means, go ahead.

Thousand dollar moments

When organizing, how do you decide what's worth keeping?

A gentleman attending one of my speeches shared his strategy. Once a month, he got rid of everything in his basement he wasn't using and could replace for five dollars or less. The risk of having to replace something if he needed to was worth it; he preferred a clutter free basement. He theorized that as he got older, he might be willing to discard items that cost as much as twenty dollars.

He was correct that his financial threshold might increase. It might even soar if something intense happened, such as an illness in the family. In those situations, priorities become clear. You recognize clutter for exactly what it is. If something as intense happened to this gentleman, he might be willing to get rid of something worth even a thousand dollars. He just wouldn't care about the "stuff."

I call such moments of clarity "thousand dollar moments." It can be helpful to visualize yourself in one when you're having trouble parting with anything, even stuff you never use. What's important to you? What would you care about in a thousand dollar moment? Knowing this can help you when getting organized.

10 Photos

When asked what they would take if they had to flee
their house, the answer most people give is the same:
the family photos. Photographs represent your life history. They are your link to previous generations and what
you browse through to recall fun times and major life
events. Organizing and protecting your collection will
allow you to enjoy your photos now and also ensure they
will be intact for future generations to inherit.

If worse comes to worst and you need to vacate your
house quickly, having all the photos in one place makes
it easy to grab the ones you want. Of course, never stop
for this in the event of a true emergency. You can get
replacement or substitute photos from friends and family.

If you're faced with the daunting task

of organizing decades worth of photos, start with the most recent first. They will be the easiest to tackle, because you'll be familiar with the people in the pictures and able to remember the locations and dates. Once you have a system established, you can incorporate the older photos into it gradually.

Look at clothing and cars for clues to dates of unlabeled photos. Photocopy or scan old family photos and send to relatives for help in identifying people you don't know. (Don't expose an original photo to the light from a scanner or copier too many times.)

Protect your photos

To ensure that cherished family photos last for years to come, shield them from elements that speed deterioration, fading and distortion.

RISK	WHAT TO DO
Light.	It's critical to store original photos in a dark place. Even putting them in a storage box or album helps. Exposure to light is one of the biggest causes of damage.
Temperature and humidity.	Avoid storing photos in the attic, basement or garage. These areas are prone to environmental extremes and fluctuations. Choose a space in the main part of your house, such as a spare closet.
Water.	Don't store where you've had, or could have, water leaks. Specifically avoid storing in cardboard boxes on your basement floor; one burst washing machine hose could soak them all. Also, try not to eat and drink near where you're sorting and organizing photos so as to not risk a spill.
Handling.	Hold photographs by the edges when viewing them. Take care not to bend them. Wear clean cotton gloves when assembling albums to prevent fingerprints and dirt from getting on the face of the photos.

Safe storage products

Purchase photo organizing supplies made of materials that won't harm your prints. Appropriate products aren't hard to find—check photography or scrapbooking catalogs and websites, storage and organization stores, and office supply outlets.

* When purchasing albums, scrapbooks or other photo storage, look for these key words on the packaging: "archival," "archival quality" or "archival safe."

* Avoid "magnetic" photo albums, those that require you to peel back clear plastic from a sticky cardboard page to insert photos. Over time, these materials can cause significant photo discoloration.

* If your album contains plastic sheet protectors or clear photo pocket pages, they should be polyvinylchloride-free (PVC-free). PVC is harmful to prints. Choose instead ones made out of such material as polypropylene or polyester.

* Any paper products, such as scrapbook pages, should be acid-free and lignin-free. (Lignin is a natural by-product of wood that can be damaging to photographic material.)

"Getting organized is not about getting rid of your memories.

It's about making them more accessible."

Treat blurry or otherwise inferior photos like you would junk mail: pitch or delete immediately. Just because you took a picture doesn't mean you have to keep it. In fact, the less photo clutter you have, the easier it is to enjoy the great shots.

Photo box system for storage

The fastest, most consistent method of organizing prints is to use a photo box with archival envelopes. There are kits available commercially that include the photo box, twenty-five archival photo envelopes, CD or negative sleeves, duplicate number stickers and an indexing card.

1. Place a set of prints into one of the kit's envelopes. If you had the prints developed professionally, toss any leftover store packaging.

2. On the front of the envelope, record pertinent information such as date, location, event and attendees.

3. Record the same information on the photo box index. By filling this in each time you add a set of prints, you will create a master list of what's in the box.

4. If you have CDs or negatives, slip them into the protective sleeves.

5. Place one of the number stickers on the photo envelope and the duplicate to that sticker on the CD/negative sleeve. If you decide to reprint a photo, you'll know exactly where to find the negative or digital copy.

6. File the envelope in the photo box. Store CDs and negatives separately as a backup. Potential locations include a fireproof box, a safe deposit box or at a relative's house.

✳ # On the outside, a photo album and a scrapbook look essentially the same. The difference is in what you do inside.

IN A PHOTO ALBUM, you display just the pictures. You can mount them onto paper or cardstock. Or you can slip them into photo pocket pages configured with either four 3 ½ x 5-inch (9 cm x 13 cm), three 4 x 6-inch (10 cm x 15 cm), or two 5 x 7-inch (13 cm x 18 cm) pockets.

IN A SCRAPBOOK, you try to tell the story behind the pictures. To do this, write your thoughts about an event and include them with the photos. Also incorporate memorabilia such as tickets, programs and brochures. Add stickers and borders to make it decorative.

Don't stress about albums

You don't have to put all of your photographs in scrapbooks or albums for them to be organized. In fact, using such a portfolio for all of them can be time-consuming, expensive and require a lot of storage space. If you do want to pursue this display option, remember it's perfectly acceptable to create just a few books, such as one for each child's school years or one commemorating a special vacation.

Over- or odd-sized photos, including those of your ancestors, can lie flat in an archival storage box.

Mounting photos or memorabilia on a page

Use this technique to include an item in an album or scrapbook when you want to preserve its original condition and don't want it permanently attached to the page.

1. Purchase a box of mounting corners. These triangular-shaped pockets have a sticky back so you can attach them to a page, and are open along one edge so you can slide the corner of an item into them.

2. Decide where on the page the photo or memorabilia will be located.

3. Affix four mounting corners to the page, one each where a corner of the item will rest.

4. Insert each corner of the item into a corner mount. Your photo or memorabilia will be held securely, but not permanently, in place.

If you have articles or photos

clipped from the newspaper that you want to include in a scrapbook, consider making a scan or a photocopy and including that copy instead. Newspaper deteriorates quickly and turns yellow because it's a low-quality, acidic paper. If you use a copy, it will last longer than the original and you can reduce or enlarge it so it's exactly the right size for your page.

You can still keep the actual newspaper articles. They're best stored flat and unfolded in an archival document box. To slow down the yellowing process, use a de-acidification solution available from professional photography and scrapbooking catalogs.

Labeling options

Note the date, event and especially the people in your photos so you and future generations can recall them in years to come.

⁂ **PHOTO BOX WITH ENVELOPES.** If you are using this system and have an envelope that contains photos all from the same event, label just the envelope with the relevant information.

⁂ **ALBUM.** Photo pocket pages often have corresponding, small pockets into which you can slip a label. This is ideal because you can indicate exactly who is in the photo above the label.

⁂ **SCRAPBOOK.** If you create scrapbooks, you have significant labeling flexibility. Use special acid-free marking pens, labels or stickers to add captions directly on your pages.

⁂ **DIGITAL.** When storing images electronically, name the computer file or folder precisely—you'll know which photos are stored there.

⁂ **WRITING ON THE PHOTOGRAPH.** If you decide to label the back of a picture, do so carefully. Use a graphite pencil and take care not to press so hard that you create ridges on the front of the image. Avoid ballpoint pen because the ink can imprint the next photo in the stack and, over time, leak through to the front of the original print.

Going digital

Digital photos offer many benefits. It's worth converting some of your favorite snapshots from years past to this format because:

※ It's cheap to share them with others by e-mailing them.

※ You can organize and reorganize them in multiple ways.

※ They can be found quickly through a keyword search.

※ You can alter, touch up or crop them.

※ They take up very little physical space.

※ It's fast to create a backup copy.

However, when taking digital photos in the future, watch out for these pitfalls:

※ With no film to purchase, photos seem free. This may lead you to take pictures without restraint, resulting in an overload of images.

※ For some people, out of sight is out of mind. Don't neglect organizing digital photos just because they're stored in your computer and you don't "see" them.

To preserve your photos

for generations to come, it's important to have a backup system.

DUPLICATE YOUR PRINTS. The best way to preserve an original print is to store it safely away. Use only a duplicate for sharing or displaying. In this way, the original serves as the backup, particularly if you don't have a negative or a digital copy of it. However, if a photo is very important to you and all you have is a print, you should scan it so you have a digital version. If you don't have a scanner, your local copy and print store can do this for you.

BACKUP ELECTRONIC FILES. If your digital photos are stored only in your computer, you risk losing them if your hard drive fails. Images should be backed up onto a removable medium (this is a general term for an electronic storage device used to move data between computers). Store the backup copy in a safe location, preferably away from your house, so that it's safe in the event of a catastrophe.

Deciding where to hang photos

Use this strategy to hang framed photographs in the right place the first time. Minimize the chance of making unnecessary holes in the wall.

1. First, lay your prints on the floor, arranged as you want them on the wall. Play with the layout and adjust the distance between items.

2. Go for balance but not necessarily absolute symmetry. You don't have to hang two prints of the same size side by side to create an appealing display. Make the wall more interesting by contrasting a large print with two smaller ones.

3. When you feel comfortable with your proposed layout, cut pieces of newspaper to the size of each frame. Lightly tape the newspaper squares to the wall where you plan to put the pictures.

4. Center your display horizontally between two focal points. Use large pieces of furniture or architectural features of the room as these "anchors."

5. When deciding how high to hang an item, remember that eye level is typically 57 to 60 inches (145 to 152 cm) from the floor.

6. Once you're satisfied with how the wall will look, lightly indicate in pencil where on the wall the top corner of each frame belongs. Then take down the newspaper squares and refer to the marks to hang the photos in their place.

Picture perfect

One of my clients had thousands of snapshots, collected over a lifetime of family events and world travel. Over the years, both the piles and the thought of organizing them grew overwhelming. At age seventy, she decided the time had come to get them in order.

We began by sorting the photos by decade. The same people appeared in photos over and over, so it became easy to recognize them and approximate how old they might be in each photo. We also had life events to work with, such as before and after she was part of a blended family. Once sorted, we stored most of the pictures in archival photo boxes with envelopes. Each envelope held the photos from one event, vacation or subject (such as children with their new puppy). The large formal portraits from her childhood years went into albums or document boxes.

We spent several weeks on the project, off and on—not a bad time investment for the decades worth of accumulation. What I learned was that this stuffed-in-the-back-of-the-closet project that weighs heavy on the minds of so many people is not as bad as you think it's going to be. Even I was surprised. We set up a system, got into a rhythm, and pretty soon we were done. So if you're procrastinating on your own photo project, remember that even seventy years' worth can be handled in a matter of weeks.

11 Children

Children have the same need to be organized that adults do. Think about it. They have academic and personal demands on their time, and on top of that they're still figuring out who they are. It's a lot to ask of a young person. But when they're organized, life is easier on them and you. They juggle schoolwork and extracurricular activities better. You relax because there are fewer manic mornings and frantic searches for missing stuff. Both of you take pleasure in having more time to spend together doing what you enjoy.

When children learn to get organized, they have skills they can use in school, in their careers and throughout their lives. Organizing principles can be learned. Now is the time to teach them to your children.

"Make organizing systems simple for children to understand and easy for them to use."

✳ **BOOST YOUR CHILDREN'S ORGANIZING SKILLS** with this concept: everybody needs a home. Help them designate a place where each toy lives. They understand the reasoning behind "knowing where you live so you don't get lost."

✳ **BUY SHALLOW STORAGE BINS** for toys so kids don't have to empty them out to get at what's in the bottom. Let your children pick out and decorate their own storage containers. The more they like their system, the more likely they are to use it.

✳ **EVEN IF CONTAINERS ARE SEE-THROUGH**, be sure to label them. Your children will know where to find toys and where to put them back if the contents are clearly identified. If you have youngsters who can't read yet, tape a picture to the container.

A closet for all ages and stages

You expect to buy new clothes and shoes as your youngsters grow, but not entire new closet systems. Yet as they mature, children's storage needs change. An adjustable closet can be reconfigured as needed.

1. Choose an adjustable closet system that has components such as rods, shelves and drawers available.

2. Look for one that's easy to install. The best require you to drill holes only for one horizontal track that goes near the ceiling.

3. When your child is young, configure the closet with at least two rods. The bottom one must be low enough for her to hang up everyday clothes.

4. Reserve higher rods for special occasion or seasonal garments.

5. When your child gets taller, remove the lower rod.

6. In its place, add other accessories such as drawer units and shoe stackers.

7. If you have a teenage daughter, leave enough space for dresses and long skirts to hang without brushing anything below.

If you restructure closets as your children age, you'll maximize both your space and your investment in the system.

Manage morning mania by setting aside time on Sundays for kids to select school clothes for the whole week. Organize entire outfits on five hangers labeled Monday – Friday.

✳

Small children can dress themselves if you buy only clothes that fasten in the front. Remember, zippers and snaps are easier than buttons for little fingers.

✳

Have children get their backpacks together before bedtime. Don't leave this task until after breakfast when everyone is rushing to get out the door.

The upside to putting up toys

When the number of toys underfoot overwhelms you (and your children), establish a rotation schedule. Note the ones they currently play with the most, leave these out, and put the rest away in the attic or the basement. After a few months, put more toys away and bring others out. The benefits to both of you are:

❊ There are fewer toys to make a mess.

❊ Children are more likely to focus and play creatively if not distracted by too many choices.

❊ When you bring back toys they haven't seen in a while, it is like something "new" to play with.

❊ Getting additional toys from your attic instead of the store can save you a lot of money in the long run.

USE A FELT-TIP MARKER to put the same number on the back of each piece from the same puzzle. Use a different number for each puzzle you have. Pieces won't get mixed in with the wrong puzzle.

TINY TOYS (small cars, miniature airplanes, palm-sized plastic animals) should be stored in a container no larger than a shoebox. Otherwise, there will be extra room in the container and your child will be tempted to toss unrelated items in on top.

STORE BOOKS belonging to a young child in a series of plastic tubs. This will allow him room to flip each book forward so he can see the cover, as this is how young ones often identify their books. It's much harder to see the covers if books are stored upright on a shelf. Turn them in the tub so the spines are facing up. It's easier for him to riffle through if all the books aren't falling open.

Think outside the (toy)box

Ordinary household items can be converted into kids' storage units.

✳ **PICNIC TABLE UTENSIL HOLDERS** – Designed to separate forks, spoons and knives, these are usually divided into
four to six compartments. They work well for organizing craft
supplies such as markers, crayons and paintbrushes.

✳ **OVER-THE-DOOR POCKET BAGS** – Choose one with clear
pockets. Instead of putting it in the clothes closet for shoes,
hang it in the hall closet so hats and gloves are within kids'
reach. Or place it in the bathroom to corral barrettes, ponytail
scrunchies and hair ribbons.

✳ **NAIL AND SCREW ORGANIZERS** – Found in hardware
stores, these storage units have anywhere from eight to
sixty-four tiny drawers. They're perfect for storing childhood
treasures such as pebbles, shells and stickers.

✳ **SHOE CUBBIES** – Children like these wooden units because
they're open and everything is visible. Instead of shoes, use
them for stuffed animals or other small toys.

To encourage children to participate

in household chores, hand out age-appropriate assignments. When they struggle with a task beyond their ability level, it's frustrating for both of you. Consider letting them select their tasks from a list of all that needs to be done so they feel like they have a say in the matter.

* **Provide** clear instruction. Saying "please clean your room" doesn't provide enough direction for children to know where to start. Nor will they be able to gauge when they're finished. More effective: request that they drop their dirty clothes in the hamper and tuck dolls into bed.

* **Explain** not only what the chore is, but also why your child should do it. What are the benefits to her? If her room is picked up, will she have more time to play, be able to find the toy she's looking for and protect her dolls from getting stepped on and dirty? If she perceives the benefits to be important to her, she will be more likely to do the task.

* **Model** behavior by doing your "homework" at the same time they do theirs. An added bonus: working side by side, you'll serve as motivators for each other and you'll both get done faster.

Time management for kids

When teaching time management to a child, use an ana-log clock (one where the hands move around in a circle) rather than a digital clock. Time is easier for them to conceptualize when they can see the minutes moving by.

A signal that your child is old enough to learn to plan is that he begins to receive long-term homework assign-ments. Have him record the due date on a month-at-a-glance calendar. Then have him establish interim dead-lines and note those on the calendar too.

It can be difficult for very young children to budget time, so break their chores into ten- or fifteen-minute blocks. Use a kitchen timer to signal the end of each segment.

Teenagers use their bedrooms for three different activities: studying, socializing and sleeping.

For one room to accommodate all three functions, it's best to use multipurpose furniture. Decorative wooden cubes provide a place for files and can also serve as a coffee table when your child has friends over. Storage ottomans hold blankets and can be used as extra seating when needed. A daybed can be both a couch and a place to sleep.

Create a study center in your home

Just as a business person has an office with a desk, a student needs an area where he can study and store his schoolwork. Follow these five steps to establish order:

1. Set up a work surface. It can be a desk or a large table. There should be enough space for both paperwork and a computer, as well as an accessible power outlet.

2. Find a chair that is at the right height for the table. Your child may need a footstool to maintain proper posture.

3. Bring in task lighting. A desk or floor lamp that shines on the work surface will do.

4. Label one hanging file folder for each class. If there is no file drawer, use a portable file box to house them.

5. Create a basket containing all the frequently used supplies such as pens, pencils and stapler.

Avoid using the kitchen table as the study center, loading it up with backpacks, books and supplies. It's disruptive to children to have to move all their work when it's time to eat dinner. If mom or dad need to supervise homework while cooking, have your child bring just a few papers to the kitchen table or island to work on.

Locker basics

A locker is basically a closet, only at school. Just like your bedroom closet would be hard to organize if it didn't have shelves, rods and hangers, a locker can quickly become a mess if not equipped with the right accessories. Any products that you add should be sturdy, yet temporary and removable.

- **SHELVES.** Removable ones sized just for a locker are available. Position one or two in the top third of the locker and store books and lunch there. Use the space below for backpacks, gym clothes and musical instruments.

- **BINS.** At a minimum, affix one large and two small bins to the inside of the door. Use the large one for spiral notebooks or a planner. Use the smaller ones for pens, pencils, keys, pocket change and other small items.

- **HOOKS.** Add more if there aren't already enough in the locker. Hang coats, backpack and umbrella.

- **MESSAGE BOARD.** A magnet-backed dry erase board provides a spot to jot important thoughts that come to mind between classes.

To grandmother's house we go

Do you have preschoolers who frequently get to spend the night at their grandparents' house? Purchase duplicate pajamas, toothbrushes, and other necessities for over there. It's much quicker to get them ready if you don't have to pack these every time.

When you travel by plane with a baby or toddler, bringing a change of clothing for them is a given. But don't forget another shirt for yourself, a necessity in the event of a spill when you're holding them.

When storing your children's outgrown clothing

for potential hand-me-downs, organize it according to the approximate weight your child was when he wore the outfits. Baby clothes sizes vary, so this is a more accurate way of sorting the clothes. Label the storage boxes accordingly by gender and weight.

What to do with children's artwork

Overwhelmed with the art your children create every day? Not sure what to do with it? You have four options:

❋ **DISPLAY.** Only a few pieces should be chosen to display. Decide where you'll do this (on the refrigerator, tacked to a bulletin board or framed and hung in the hallway). Make a plan for rotating the pictures. You may refresh the refrigerator display every week, but frame other "masterpieces" and leave them up for years.

❋ **MAIL.** What you've chosen to mail to grandparents and other admirers should be sent on its way quickly. A personal note on the back or a signature from the artist makes it that much more special. Most artwork can also be laminated and made into placemats that grandparents will treasure. You can scan twelve drawings and have them made into a photo-a-month calendar. Both make great holiday gifts.

❋ **DISCARD.** Having a hard time narrowing the rest down to a few pieces you want to retain? Keep it all until the end of the semester, then reevaluate. With the passage of time and the benefit of seeing it all together, it's easier to determine what represents a significant milestone in your child's development or is a truly unique creation.

❋ **STORE.** Make sure you have the right containers for storing art you don't display. Insects and water are your two biggest enemies. Avoid cardboard boxes and choose plastic instead. Art supply stores have large, flat portfolios that are perfect for oversized paintings.

An artist creates an album

I was invited to speak to a group of young mothers about organizing their homes and lives. The conversation eventually turned to talk of arts and crafts. Specifically, how to cope with the sheer volume of projects and paintings that children turn out, both at school and home.

One of the mothers was an artist. She shared the solution she had developed years earlier. Once a month, she had each child select their favorite project from the past four weeks. She photographed the child with their art and these photos went into an Art Album. With only twelve photos per child per year, she had room for several years' worth in each child's album. The majority of the actual art, unless it went to grandparents, was eventually recycled or discarded.

The albums were more meaningful to her than the actual art. With the pictures, she had a record of her children growing up and their work becoming more sophisticated. It was her heart-warming and clutter-free solution.

12 Holidays

Holidays are a special time of year. They're also a busy time. To enjoy the festivities and family gatherings, plan ahead of time how you'll work in the extra responsibilities that accompany the holiday season. Because the same activities happen annually (decorating shopping, entertaining, family activities), you can set up routines and checklists that will benefit you year after year.

Consciously planning and organizing at this time of year will help you save money on gifts and travel. Plus, you won't have to worry about accidentally leaving someone off your list and causing hurt feelings. Best of all, you can enjoy the celebrations without feeling frazzled.

Before heading out to do holiday shopping,

organize your gift list by store (not by person). You'll be less likely to forget anything at a particular outlet and have to backtrack. Begin at the store farthest from your house. That way, if you don't finish, what's left is close by.

PRESSED FOR GIFTS AT THE LAST MINUTE? If you're traveling by plane to your holiday destination and either arrive at the airport early to get through security or have a layover in another city, shop at the upscale airport stores. Many airports now make assurances that their stores' prices are no higher than what you would find at the mall. Purchase only gifts that fit inside your carry-on luggage or (if you can carry on additional packages) in the overhead bin or under the seat in front of you.

Refer to this

CREATE A WALLET-SIZED CARD that lists the clothing sizes of each family member. This is incredibly helpful to have with you when shopping. Kept in your billfold, it's also quick to find when grandparents ask for this information.

ANOTHER USEFUL REFERENCE CARD to carry is one with your home's room dimensions and window sizes. When shopping for curtains, rugs or furniture, you can check immediately to see if an item will fit.

Set up a wrapping station with paper, bows, scissors and tape. Choose an out-of-the-way location so you can leave the supplies sitting out through the season. Wrap a few gifts each evening to prevent a last-minute all-nighter.

❄

To save time writing gift tags, designate a different colored wrapping paper for each child's gifts. Keep the code to yourself and no one will know which gifts are his. It will heighten the surprise.

❄

Once presents are covered snugly in paper and topped with a festive bow, arrange them artfully in your living room. Do this even with gifts that you will mail or hand deliver to friends. The colorful packages stacked together will add extra holiday cheer to your home.

❄

At the end of the season, store your holiday paper and gift bags with your decorations. Because you won't need this specially-themed wrapping the rest of the year, there's no need to store it with your other gift wrap supplies.

Make a list and check it twice

Lists can keep you sane, particularly during the holidays. Here are good ones to make at this time of year.

IDEA LIST	Include people to whom you'll give a present and corresponding gift ideas. You can list several possibilities and purchase the first you find or the one that best fits within your budget.
WISH LIST	It's okay to write down ideas for gifts you'd like to receive (Just in case someone asks!).
THANK YOU'S	Note what gifts you have received. Leave a space to check off when the thank-you note has been written.
MASTER REFERENCE	This is a comprehensive final list of what you gave and to whom. Use it as a reference next year.
CARDS	Create a list of holiday greetings received and sent. Also keep your address book up to date.
PARTY PLANNING	Plan ahead with menus and grocery lists for parties you're hosting. When guests offer to bring one of the planned dishes, accept the help. This will lessen the pressure on you.

Get shopping done quickly

❋ Shop when the stores are least crowded: right when they open and again at dinner time.

❋ Call ahead to see if a boutique has what you're looking for.

❋ Use a complimentary personal shopping service if it's offered.

❋ Purchase online or via catalog.

❋ Come up with a gift theme for the year—books, for example—and you can limit your shopping to one or two stores.

Prepare a list of non-perishable food items

you need for your holiday feast and make an early visit to the grocery store. At least some of your shopping can be done in advance of the most crowded days. Save shopping for perishables like produce or fresh seafood until a day or two ahead of your event.

When shopping by catalog or internet

it's best to allow extra time in case any of the items you want are back-ordered or arrive but need to be exchanged for a different size or color. On the flip side, if you're willing to risk the desired item not being in stock and you're prepared to pay a premium for shipping, many of these outlets will let you place an order right at the last minute.

Realize that during the holidays, you may receive several copies of the same catalog, just with different covers. You only need to keep one copy.

Including individual notes in each holiday card you send takes time. It would be difficult to complete them all in an evening. However, you can address all the envelopes in one sitting. That way, you won't forget anyone, even if you spread the job out over a month, and you'll prevent doubling up on anyone.

As you receive holiday cards, check whether your friend or relative has a new address. If so, save the envelope. Use it to update your address book during a quiet evening after the holidays.

If you start at the end of November and write just two notes a night, you can send almost seventy-five greetings by the New Year!

 If you have too many other tasks on your list for December, start a tradition of sending New Year greetings instead.

Fast and festive decorating

It's possible to jazz up your home without dragging out all your decorations. If you just have a small window of time, you can:

* Run a string of colored lights around each mirror in each room. They'll reflect, so you'll get twice the twinkle for minimal effort. Whenever you want to create a warm glow, turn off all the overhead lights and illuminate the rooms with only these tiny lights.

* Use hooks with removable adhesive to hang pine-scented wreaths and garland. Because you can remove these special hooks without marring the walls, you can hang the decorations quickly and fearlessly.

* Tie a gold or silver bow around each throw pillow so they look like gift packages.

* "Wrap" some of the artwork that normally hangs on your walls by covering it with festive holiday paper. Attach bows and ribbons for an instant wall of presents.

* Settle on one major focal point such as an elaborate dining room table centerpiece. If you go all out in one area, the absence of other decorations will go unnoticed.

Love how you decorated your house this season?

Take a minute to preserve your ideas for next year. Photograph the mantel, centerpiece and anything else that turned out well. Place the pictures in an envelope and tuck them inside one of your holiday storage boxes.

This will serve as a decorating guide for the next holiday season, reminding you how many candles you prefer on the mantel and the number of staircase spindles to leave between each loop of garland.

Card control

To organize the holiday cards you receive and enjoy them at the same time, use them to decorate.

- ✳ Temporarily take down your wall décor, hang an empty bulletin board in its spot, and tack up incoming cards.

- ✳ Loop a ribbon from a windowsill. Suspend cards by running the ribbon up under the fold of each card. As your collection grows, you'll create a garland effect.

- ✳ Use cards to make a collage viewable through a glass top coffee table. Reach underneath and tape cards to the glass. Begin at the edges, where the thick glass rests on the frame. Create a border first and work your way to the middle as you receive more greetings.

- ✳ Create colorful archways by lining door frames with the cards you receive.

Place a large plastic tarp

on the floor before positioning the stand and tree. (Once you add your tree skirt it will be hidden.) It will catch any accidental drips that occur when you water the tree. At the end of the season, spread out the tarp and lay the tree down on it as you remove it from the stand. Pull the tarp up around the tree and carry it outside this way. You'll prevent loose needles from making a mess in the house.

Protect your décor

Good storage protects your decorations and makes it faster to both get them out and put them away each year.

1. Choose appropriate containers. There are totes of different sizes that are perfect for garlands and tinsel, boxes with dividers to protect ornaments, and specialized cases for everything from artificial trees to seasonal wreaths.

2. Consider purchasing containers that are all the same color so they will be easy to spot in your storage room.

3. Wrap heirloom ornaments and holiday dishes in plain packing paper or acid-free tissue (available from storage and organization stores or Christmas supply outlets). Avoid using newspaper because the ink can damage your treasures.

4. Affix an inventory to the outside of each box as you pack items away. In future years, your inventories will make quick work of retrieving the decorations you want. Plus, putting them away will be a snap because you'll know what fits in each tote.

How to organize your stored decorations

The best way to organize and store your holiday decorations is according to how you'll retrieve them next year.

- ❊ **ROOM** — Do you put together a room at a time? Group together everything for that space.

- ❊ **CATEGORY** — Is your preference to decorate in stages: garland one day, lights the following one? Opt for the category choice.

- ❊ **COLOR** — Do you rotate your décor, grabbing what's gold one year and selecting what's silver the next? You should organize according to color.

Lights on

Always plug in a string of lights before placing them on the tree or hanging them outside your house. You want to know if the strand is working before going to this effort. To prevent having to search a string for the one non-working light bulb, buy strands that stay lit even if one bulb is burned out.

String your tree lights from top to bottom, rather than around in a circle. They'll be easier to remove later than if you have to walk around and around the tree to do so.

To keep them from getting tangled when stored, wind each strand around an empty wrapping paper tube. (Cut tubes in half or thirds depending on how long your strands are.) Make a slit in the end of the tube and anchor the plug there. Lay them in storage boxes; use separate ones for indoor versus outdoor lights.

TRAVELING TO SPEND TIME WITH FAMILY? Hold off on wrapping gifts you plan to carry on an airplane. Security personnel may need to look inside the packages. Instead, measure the amount of wrapping paper you'll need and tuck it inside the box.

PREFER TO TRAVEL LIGHT? Bring "envelope gifts"—gift certificates, subscription notices, entertainment tickets—anything that fits into an envelope.

The organized guest room

A cozy bedroom is a treasure on a brisk winter night. Your company will appreciate:

> ❊ A bedside reading lamp and an alarm clock, drinking glasses and a water carafe, storage spot for luggage, clothing valet, extra blankets placed on a chair or at the bottom of the bed, a note about House Rules (for instance, "Help yourself to anything in the fridge").

A luxurious guest bath is a welcome sight to weary travelers. Pamper them with:

> ❊ Fluffy towels set out just for them on their own towel rack, a fresh box of tissues, a shower caddy for their shampoo and conditioner, a magazine rack and reading material and hooks for their bathrobes.

Nothing is so relaxing as an uncluttered closet. Visitors will love opening the door to:

> ❊ An ample supply of elegant hangers, shoe organizers or cubbies, clothing steamer or iron and ironing board on a holder, sewing kit, shoe care kit.

A family gathering

is the perfect time to share family history and tales of the past. Make an audio or video recording of the storytelling. The anecdotes can be transcribed later and bound into book format for each family member.

You can also ask timely questions, such as the most memorable thing that happened to each person this year. If you follow this format each time you're together for the holidays, you'll have a rich, historical record to pass down to the next generation.

Your Organized Life

You may not realize it, but you're already organizing every day. You're constantly making decisions about what to do with your time and your stuff. The question is whether or not what you're doing is working for you. If it is, stick with it. If it's not, then take advantage of the opportunity to organize differently.

Having read this book, you have new ideas, explanations and ways of looking at things. You've refreshed your memory about the benefits of having less clutter and have the motivation to move forward.

Take from this book what works for you. Use the ideas in various rooms of your home; apply the concepts in multiple situations. After all, organizing is not something you do once and you're done. An organized life is a way of living.

resources

With appreciation to the following companies whose products are shown in this book:

PAGES 2 AND 185:
Lookers® Square Boxes
Design Ideas Ltd.
www.designideas.net
800-426-6394

PAGE 8:
Viola Drawer Organizers
The Container Store
www.containerstore.com
888-266-8246

PAGE 10:
Portabella Basket
Levenger
www.levenger.com
800-667-8034

PAGE 28:
Hanging File Folders
Smead Manufacturing Company
www.smead.com
651-437-4111

PAGE 28:
LetraTag Labels
DYMO Corporation
www.dymo.com
800-426-7827

PAGE 46:
Hangers
Hangers.Com
www.hangers.com
800-400-6680

COVER AND PAGE 82:
Snap Journal and Key Chain
Designers Guild
www.designersguild.com

PAGE 98:
Under-Bed Box
Rubbermaid Home Products
www.rubbermaid.com
888-895-2110

PAGE 114:
31 Day Monthly Bill Organizer
IN2 Products
www.in2products.com
800-746-3048

PAGE 137:
Crunch® Can
Umbra
www.umbra.com
800-387-5122

PAGE 146:
Craftsman Tool Chest
Sears
www.sears.com
800-349-4358

PAGE 162:
TrueCore™ Flat Storage Boxes
Light Impressions
www.lightimpressionsdirect.com
800-828-6216

PAGE 178:
GO-Box™ Cubby
Schulte Corporation
www.schultestorage.com
800-669-3225

PAGE 210:
Red Holiday Box
The Container Store
www.containerstore.com
888-266-8246

index

THE RIGHT WAY
Guidelines for Good Behavior
Lauren McCutcheon

There is a right way and a wrong way to do things—from mowing the lawn to entering a revolving door. Avoid social gaffes by referring to the informative diagrams and helpful hints in this lovely little guide. Find *The Right Way* to handle any scenario!
ISBN: 1-58297-465-9,
978-1-58297-465-1,
$9.99 pb, 128 p, #Z0424

HANDBAGS
What Every Woman Should Know
Stephanie Pederson

Shoes? Jewelry? Those are wonderful, of course, but sometimes only handbags—multiple handbags—will do the job. Do purses from Marc Jacobs, Prada, Hermès make you shiver? Can a vintage 'Jackie O Bag' make you moan?

Tuck this little guide to every woman's secret passion into your purse and pursue your pleasure.
ISBN: 0-7153-2495-0,
ISBN 13: 978-0-7153-2495-0,
$12.99 hc, 128 p, #41890

GUT
How to Think from Your Middle to Get to the Top
Karen Salmansohn

With *Gut*, discover the key to making amazingly smart and beneficial decisions on a daily basis by listening to your highest level of knowing—gut instincts. Wise decisions are always based on being attracted to opportunity, priorities and high values, as Karen Salmansohn knows. Tap into instincts and conquer your fears and self doubt with *Gut*!
ISBN: 1-58180-817-8,
ISBN 13: 978-1-58180-817-9,
$14.99 pb, 208 p, #33497